Christianity
in a Culture of Conflict

Christianity in a Culture of Conflict

Six Addresses

Clifford E. Bajema

Dordt College Press

Copyright © 2007 by **Clifford E. Bajema**

Fragmentary portions of this book may be freely used by those who are interested in sharing this aging author's insights and musings, so long as the material is not pirated for monetary gain and so long as proper credit is visibly given to the publisher and the author. Others, and those who wish to use larger sections of text, must seek written permission from the publisher.

Printed in the United States of America.

Dordt College Press
498 Fourth Avenue NE
Sioux Center, Iowa 51250
United States of America
ISBN-13: 978-0-932914-77-4

www.dordt.edu/dordt_press

Cover design by Robert Haan

The Library of Congress Cataloging-in-Publication Data is on file with the Library of Congress, Washington, D.C.

Library of Congress Control Number: 2007927317

Contents

Foreword i
    James Calvin Schaap

1. "Oh My God!"—America's Culture of Irreverence 1

2. The Christian Mind Rediscovered 11

3. Christianity in Culture: Three Paths 23

4. Postmodernist Culture and the Christian Mind 33

5. Christianity and Secular Humanism 41

6. Our Culture of Impermanence and Our Unchanging God . 61

Foreword

In retrospect, his two semesters out here in Siouxland seems almost mythic—a prophet with a silver mane, riding in on a Harley like some reverend Lone Ranger, a poet in black leather boots, a striking presence behind a podium, a man big enough to cry, and do so publicly. He lived on campus, supped with students, loved stories, told them well, and deeply missed his wife back east. Creative and even rebellious by nature, he could be deadly serious and sober as a judge but never quite beyond a grand belly laugh. In the year he spent on the Dordt College campus, he gave us his heart and soul; but his first love was always the Lord God almighty.

The Reverend Clifford Bajema came to Dordt College to lead worship. He came because we needed him, and so did the ancient rite of Tuesday and Thursday chapel, the twice-weekly worship experiences that had been a part of campus life for, right then, exactly fifty years.

Chapel had fallen on hard times. Attendance was dropping, interest failing. Those of us who've been to Dordt College chapels for many years have seen all kinds of shows, heard all kinds of presentations: hundreds of sermons and dozens of sales pitches for all kinds of worthy organizations, to be sure. For a while dormitory floors were in charge—a fiasco. Voices from off-campus offered meditations, but the line-up of strange faces started to feel like the old who's-on-first shtick. Students, profs—chapel committees have tried just about everything.

Just a few years before he came, students had determined to do their own thing. Hundreds of them came together religiously on Sunday and Wednesday nights for praise-and-worship fests, stood together on their feet for an hour, their hands raised in praise, a kind of Dordt College Great Awakening. When Cliff Bajema came to town, there was no dearth of piety on campus; but its abundance didn't show itself in chapel.

Some saw chapel as a meeting ground, a sort of middle-of-the-road worship event, deftly placed between relatively staid Sunday worship in local churches and the rock concert environment of Sunday night GIFT (Growing in Faith Together) gatherings. Some saw Dordt chapel as a dinosaur, a worn-out ritual whose time had come and gone, like bobby socks and penny loafers, peace signs and headbands, a gasping relic of by-gone religiosity.

Faculty tolerated chapel, but rarely attended GIFT services. Students flooded GIFT but shrugged off chapel. Our seams were stretched and splitting, a gaping divide separating generations; and all the while, chapel crowds grew ever leaner.

Some argued that it was time for the college to require chapel attendance; after all, our neighbors down the road in Orange City did, as does Wheaton, not to mention dozens of other Christian colleges. The sparse crowds at chapel became a public relations fiasco, the thin crowds an embarrassment. Visiting parents and prospective students raised eyebrows; some on campus even argued that such unenthusiastic attendance was a sacrilege.

Those who abandon principle at Dordt College are soon shown the way out of town, so traditionalists—those who felt chapel simply had to be voluntary—came out of the woodwork in response, foursquare against mandatory chapel attendance. No one had ever forced students to attend worship at Dordt College, they said (even though some of us remembered otherwise in days of old). Mandatory chapel seemed somehow a violation of sphere sovereignty or some other Kuyperian principle. Can you force people to worship the Lord? Required chapel started to look like an abandonment of Reformed doctrine.

That's when Cliff Bajema came rolling up on his Harley. Perhaps it's no wonder he seems mythic.

He brought a different approach to chapel, worship itself draped and garlanded anew around passionate dialogue with the God of scripture—and the God of creation. His poet's heart spoke in measured language, in formal, well-wrought prayers. He cared not only how things were said, but what was said. He tried to blend generations by finding a new voice, part praise-and-worship and part old-time gospel hymnody. He wasn't afraid to point fingers from the podium, and yet chapel worship nurtured meditation by something new—enriched silence. His own preaching was often deeply introspective and devotional.

Then and now, the campus religious climate—not unlike the cultural climate in which we breath—is an odd mix, as desirous of deep spiritual experience as it is disgusted with formal religion. *Spirituality* is the glow in Moses' face when he came down from meeting God on the mountain; *religion* is the heavy stone tablets he carried along under his arm. Today, we long for the glow, but the commandments make us nervous.

The majority culture on the Dordt College campus, the Dutch Reformed, has traditionally loved "pulpiteers," men (exclusively) who can orate, who can "hold forth," who can speak with a level of *gravitas* that makes an audience believe they are hearing the voice of an Old Testament God. It's a fine theory if Winston Churchill is in the pulpit.

Cliff Bajema brought votive candles to the B.J. Haan Auditorium. He brought dimmed lights and banners. He brought setting and silence. He brought spirituality to a people who never really knew what they'd missed until they'd experienced it. He brought art to worship, an economy of words. He brought—or tried to bring—an experience which would bring a glow to the faces of those who were there. He did something new.

Which is not to say that he himself disappeared from the experience of chapel. Few speakers ever weighed in as prophetically about all kinds of national and local topics as he did during his time here. He held forth. He was here for two semesters, our guest— and he knew that his limited time with us gave him unique opportunities, not only to minister to our needs in a priestly way, but also to draw on the biblical rhetoric of Isaiah and Jeremiah. There were times when no one sat comfortably on the padded pews.

More than anything, perhaps, it was the writer in Cliff Bajema, the artist, that created the mood in Dordt College chapels that year—not only in the manner by which he created an ambience for worship, nor simply in the sheer delight by which he crafted his sermon mediations. Memorable writing is never predictable, and neither were his chapels. None of us—students or faculty and staff would ever dare to presume exactly what might happen on Tuesday or Thursday morning in worship at the BJ Haan, and so we wanted to know. We wanted to be there.

No one would be happier than Cliff if this story would end with the full reformation of chapel worship at Dordt College. The truth is, attendance isn't soaring these days. The old question is still with us—should attendance be mandatory? On that one, the jury is still out. Our problems remain. Our character, as children of Adam, hasn't changed a bit.

But most of us who were here the year that Clifford Bajema was with us will not forget the experience of chapels because what was done there and what was said there didn't stay in the auditorium when we walked away. His meditations pursued us down the sidewalk, back into our offices and classrooms; the experiences he created for us with the God who is so beyond us that he plays with solar systems as if they were key rings—those experiences weren't left behind.

That God Cliff Bajema helped us to see during his time here. That God he helped us to know. He renewed in us that most significant of emotions for a believer, a sense of awe.

You'll see and hear and feel something of that in this book of his. The story of his time here isn't in the meditations he's giving us, but what he did is inherent in the craft of these essays and poems and meditations.

For a wonderful year, full of love and passion and grace, the entire Dordt College community owes him, and the God he serves so passionately, our grateful thanks.

James Calvin Schaap
Department of English
April 20, 2007

1

"Oh My God!"—
America's Culture of Irreverence

The face of Muhammad is reduced to an irreverent cartoon in a Danish newspaper, and the Muslim community is up in arms. The visage of Christ is depicted as dipped in urine in an art piece subsidized by the National Endowment for the Arts and Humanities, and the Christian community (with the exception of a few Fundamentalists) hardly responds. The name of God in the Western world becomes a trivial cliché, and neither Jew nor Christian challenges this irreverence.

"Oh-ma-god!"

"Oh . . . my . . . god!"

"Oh my gaawwd!!!"

Whenever someone is surprised, shaken, stunned, or smitten with self-importance, the convenient exclamatory response is inevitably "Oh my God!"

There is an accident, an unexpected phone call from a friend, a bad grade, the pleasant taste of a brownie, the bombing of the World Trade Center, a football touchdown, a look in the mirror at one's early morning face—and the first words out of one's mouth are "Oh my God!"

I wonder what this means. Is it just an in-vogue expression? A way of showing how culturally "with it" we are? A way to fit in with three mindless words? Is it just a kind of unconscious fallback when we feel something and need to give that emotion an exclamatory outlet? Is "Oh my God!" simply an expression containing three harmless words that could be easily exchanged with any other three harmless words? Like, "Oh my goodness," or "Oh my gosh," or "Oh by golly"? But why all the *g*s? Because we are too hypocritical to just say "Oh my God!"?

I wonder whether people could be convinced to use a different name combined with "Oh my," such as "Oh my Sarah," or "Oh my George," or "Oh my Jessica," or "Oh my James"? Would this work for them? Or would they be fearful of offending someone with that name?

Of course, some people don't believe that there is a God. So why, I wonder, do these very same people say his name so much? It makes no sense to me to keep referring to someone who doesn't exist!

But, for the sake of clarity and sincerity of word usage, suppose that there is a God? Would one who believed in such a deity think it flattering to use his name so vulgarly and cavalierly? How did the ancient God-worshippers, the Israelites, regard the use of God's name? Exodus 20:7 and 33:18–34:9 answer that question for us. The third commandment forbade them from taking the name of the LORD their God in vain. They could not even have the name (in the Hebrew, *JHWH*) on their lips. The name means "I AM," and when translated into English, it appears as "LORD." This was because the Hebrew scribes placed the vowels of the Hebrew word for "LORD" (*Adonai*) under the four consonants *JHWH*. They did this because, out of reverence, they would say "Adonai" whenever they were referring to the unmentionable *JHWH*. In some versions of the Bible, it is transliterated as "Jehovah" or "Yahweh."

To be sure, God is a more general name for the deity than the more specific LORD or Jehovah. It comes from the Hebrew plural *Elohim*. But though the name God does not rise to the same level of specialness as the redemptive covenant name *JHWH*, it is still utter profanity to use it in the "Oh my God" fashion as is current today. There is no veracity, no sincerity, and certainly no respect in the way God's name is carried into the discourse of everyday affairs. Besides, except for a few devout Jews who still read Hebrew and understand the distinctions just described, who cares whether the divine name he or she is using is general or specific. If God were the more specific name, thoughtless users would still bandy it about as carelessly and disrespectfully as they do now.

Think of God's perspective. What must he think of this favorite exclamation of the twenty-first century? Is he flattered? Why should he be, any more than you would feel honored if nearly everyone, upon the slightest impulse, uttered your name? Imagine it: I hear "Oh my Cliff" sputtered out thousands of times a day in the most thoughtless ways. Would I feel honored when someone says "Oh my Cliff!" right after they've accidentally stepped into a pile of dog doo on the sidewalk? When God hears shocked voices exclaiming "Oh my God!" when the twin towers are collapsing into rubble, should he be any more impressed than when the same expression was used but an hour earlier to express disgust about a traffic jam?

As I think back on the 9/11 tragedy these few years later, I am led to a different exclamation: "Would to God that he give us the gift to see ourselves as others see us." Do we have any capacity to see ourselves as others see us? I mean, as a nation? As a Western culture within a nation? As a Western culture that could be characterized as a culture of irreverence?

Yes, we are a free republic, enjoying the wonderful freedoms democracy brings, including the right to free speech. Yes, we are able to vote. Yes, we have the order of a rule of law. Yes, we are an immensely blessed people.

But are we the new Israel, we North Americans? Are we the blessed elect? The favored nation? The people blessed with such affluence because the incredible efforts of our work ethic have made us so deserving? Is an increase in material affluence a sure sign of God's blessing on a people, as Joel Osteen would have us believe? Is the mission of Christianity in the world one of messianic nationalism, as the Jerry Falwels and Pat Robertsons would have us believe?

Democracy has much to commend it. Freedom to vote is a great privilege. And we can only hope this freedom, expressed at the ballot box in Iraq, may bring hope to its people, and may become a realistic avenue for replacing tyranny and civil strife with a working democracy.

America seems to be on a crusade to transport its democracy and liberties beyond its borders. But, in our enthusiasm for such a cause, we must pause to consider that the will, the powers, and the freedoms of a people bring about a collective expression of culture, not just the right to vote and a participatory rule. And this is the question, then, that arises: Is our collective expression of culture something we very much want to export? In every aspect?

It is these kinds of questions, faced honestly, that may help us begin to understand why Islamic-based cultures are so threatened by our own. They may want the right to vote—yes. They do not want the tyranny of a Saddam Hussein in Iraq or the religious viciousness of the Taliban in Afghanistan. But do they want American values, with all that America has become as a collective culture, to be their very own?

Maybe if we took a long, hard look at this question, we wouldn't be so puzzled as to why the Iraqi people seem so eager to expel the very troops who gave them the freedom of the ballot box.

For they have been watching as we builders of civilization here in the West make our culture choices. And even if they didn't want to watch, American entertainers and investors and media types and tourists and products and exhibitions of lifestyle are everywhere. Yes, they have been watching as we builders of this civilization make our choices: willing our democratic liberties into tyrannies of hedonism. They watch as the public appetite turns entertainment into rituals of violent sport among muscled multimillionaire icons and turns wholesome humor into prime-time comedies of shameless indecencies and frivolous profanities. They watch as our treasured ideals of community service and compassion for humankind are slowly diminished by our competitive lust for money, power, and position, until a drastic tsunami temporarily jars us out of our apathetic immunity to world hunger, disease, and suffering.

In this increasingly globalized world, our civilization is pressing in on non-Western peoples. These peoples, by and large, haven't experienced our "enlightenment." And they are afraid of its approach. But what's to stop its so-called "progress"? If our Western culture brings greed rather than altruism; brings profit-driven Halliburton corporations rather than relief organizations, the Peace Corps, and sensitive community developers; brings oppressive Nike sweatshops instead of employment dignity and living wages, then should we wonder that Western culture is feared more than coveted?

If America transports Hollywood, Broadway, rap lyrics, teleporn, and endless commercials for curing male impotence with medical remedies that may have undesirable side effects lasting four hours, then may we wonder why an extremist, violent Al Qaeda religious band harbors trainers and trainees of terror? Of course, such terrorists need to be stopped. Of course, the United States made a positive contribution to Afghanistan when it uprooted the oppressive Taliban. The excellent novel *The Kite Runner* documents this in a powerful fashion. But can we not understand, even a little bit, how it is that the religious extremists can see themselves as holy and the West as evil? Can we not understand why they themselves feel terrorized by some of the values we seek to transport their way, values threatening perhaps the compellingly positive quality of community and family life so beautifully described in *The Kite Runner*?

If America is seen—not, to be sure, with objective fairness or without prejudice—as a land filled with affluence, road rage, Ecstasy raves, tailgate sabbath feasts at Super Bowls, casual cohabitations, bacchanalian parties, and apathy about the poor and innocent sufferers outside its borders, then should we expect to be idolized more than hated?

Do those Muslim families, directed by elders rather than by spoiled disrespectful youth and often blessed by simple lifestyles rather than cursed by the clutter of conveniences and plastic toys, really want our brand of democracy?

And how can non-Western peoples know that what they see of religion is not genuine Christianity, but American civil religion? Though sometimes we must admit to our shame that Western culture and Christianity seem the same.

Do you remember September 11, 2001? I think that it was a 911 call from God. And he wasn't asking for help. He was calling to say that we need help. We need him. We need escape from ourselves, the caricatures of our democracy, the compromises and silences of our Christian religion.

It is mostly in the West that sexuality has become a voyeuristic delight exploited beyond sensibility and decency. Do Saudis want their women to dress with open midriffs? Do Palestinian peasants want the technologies that give them a daily fare of David Letterman and Jay Leno and Madonna videos? Would a debilitating diet of daily sitcom immodesties, like *Friends*, nourish them? Do they want a twice-divorced, multimillionaire Donald Trump to accept them as apprentices in his cutthroat "You're fired!" style of business modeling? Do they want to enroll in his electronic university? Do they want to know all about his extraordinarily lavish (is it, now, three) weddings? Is he a potential American hero for them?

Does the developing world want a flood of American videos to give them sex and violence for entertainment when the real passion and blood they see spilling on their own soils every day is so terrible? Do we really think that they are in a frenzy over Brad Pitt's divorce or his subsequent affair and child out of wedlock with Angelina Jolie? Are they panting for news about Jennifer Lopez's latest or next husband, or Ben Affleck's (or is it Afflaaack's) newest Jennifer, or Wacko-Jocko Jackson's kinky, exploitive sex life with children? Do we think that they covet the lifestyles of the rich and famous or fix their fascinations on the fear factors of five bulging blondes?

Did a seismic change of consciousness occur after 9/11? Did the *Vanity Fair* of our culture end? Did we lose our interest in *Sex in the City*, in bacchanalian Super Bowls, in tireless consumerism?

Did any one of us really overcome our ethical and spiritual apathy such that we now truly take seriously what people say and do, especially if it is an "in your face" "Oh my God!"? Said Elton Trueblood in his *Foundations*:

> The third commandment does not condemn those who fail to believe; it condemns those who believe and do nothing about it. . . . What is dangerous is not intellectual atheism, which is unpopular, but mild religion, which is very popular indeed. . . . Of all the commandments (this one) hits us the hardest . . . because it reveals our life at its weakest and shows us that we cannot be saved except by a return to veracity and urgency.[1]

Taking everything into account that I have said, we must ask: Who do we think we are? God's gift to humanity? The highest and best civilization ever? Is the United States heaven on earth? No. But all of us would still far rather live in a free America than in a cage of Islamic rituals and rules in Saudi Arabia. We do not want to live in a male-dominated society where women are kept like slaves; covered with an *abaya* on every inch of their faces and bodies; are hidden away and kept from public view; are forbidden to go to the

---

1. Elton Trueblood, *Foundations for Reconstruction*, New York: Harper (1946), 32.

grocery store; have no books, theaters, concerts, or cinemas available to them; are allowed no other interests than cooking and reading the Koran; may have to share a husband with three other wives; and are subject to divorce if the husband merely says "I divorce you" three times in the presence of a witness.

Of course, we do not want to live in an intolerant society like Saudi Arabia where everything seems to be *haram* (sinful) and, if not sinful, then *abe (*shameful). However, such problems elsewhere should not blind us to our own deficiencies of culture. America is not the final answer to humanity's quest for the highest and best civilization ever.

Do not misunderstand: America is to be loved and served by its citizens. But more as Jeremiah loved Judah, not as Judah loved itself.

Does the developing world want our culture of turnover, change, impermanence? Does it want our culture of irreverence? There isn't a place in the world where you can hear "Oh my God!" more than these United States. But said with reverence? In worship? This great democracy has many cherished freedoms—most especially the freedom to say, "In God we trust." But has this trust become, in fact, no more than the trite coinage of a past memory? Has trust in God become the mandatory cliché with which all politicians end their political speeches: "God bless America?" Has trust in God become irrelevant? Has this trust become nothing more than the cool, profane expletive "Oh my God!" uttered, with attitude, on our self-absorbed way or uttered in shock as the twin towers are falling in front of our eyes?

Can we even begin to imagine a Muslim, no matter how nominal, uttering the expletive "Oh my Allah," or "Allah by Gollah," or "Allah baloney" whenever they need to express surprise or delight or disgust? Or can you imagine the immediate outburst of indignation that would come from them, with full support from the political correctness police, if the rest of us substituted such Allah exclamations for our usual "Oh my God"?

Shortly after September 11, 2001, I sat in the library mall of the University of Wisconsin in Madison listening to an endless litany of "Oh my Gods" from students passing by on their way to classes. And I wrote what follows, as a catharsis or maybe as a confession:

Oh-ma-god.
Oh . . . my . . . god!
Oh my gaawwd!!!

"In God we trust"—
not. Naaht!

Trust the green, not the four magic words.
Pick a four-lettered word
that fits us better.
Spend the silver;
buy a gumball;
hit the slots.

"God bless America." Yah!
Now there's the song to rouse
The Main Man,
The Mighty Goddess! Rah!
"God bless America!"

A time to curse
and a time to bless.
A time to kill
and a time to heal.

We've cursed well.
Let God now bless
all the good "my-God-ers"
going off to war.
Later we can heal.

In the name, we pledge allegiance.
In the name, we plight our troth.
In the name, we swear to truth.
In the name, we now proclaim
"God bless America!"
on our Jiffy signs.

How lame the name!
How tame the same.
Profane the people we?
Naw, no shame.

Delight, disgust, lust—
all fit the mod, Oh my God!
Cool thing to say, though,
when we need to say, you know,
whaaat-eh-ver.

Not that we really like the name.
God forbid!
Aw, doggone it!
There we go again!

It's so hard to get away
from that awe-ful G-word.
How we wish
we could stop saying *God*.

But, lighten up!
No harm meant.
God is good;
gods are good—all gods—
earthgods, me-gods, she-gods, no gods,
whaaat-eh-ver.

When will we be free?
Free! Free at last!
Of The Name?

THE . . . BIG . . . DOG
still hounds us,
will not be put at bay
until, with awe, we pray:
"Oh my God!
My Lord and my God!
You are my God.
Have mercy."

May God be merciful with us—to forgive and renew as we fall to our knees in national repentance. Yes, may God have mercy. The greatest threat to America today is not terrorism. The single greatest threat to America today is God. May he give us the grace to answer his 911 call with a humbler understanding of ourselves. May God mercifully call us back to reverence.

We are a great nation. There is so much about us that is good. But unless we as Christians bring the leaven of Christ's Kingdom values into our public life, the now too-naked public square will only pervert its liberties even more into a deterioration of public morals and into a general decay of virtue. Our calling is not to establish a Christian state to counteract the Muslim theocracies. Such lust for political power in the name of Christ will only lead to religious oppression and cause us to compromise the way of the cross. But neither may we silence our voices in the public realm nor yield the sway of our culture over to the enticements of secular entertainments, ideologies, and spirits.

We must love our Lord and love our nation enough not to let that happen. We must be the noblest spirits of our time and not view the cultural state of things as utterly hopeless. Society can be reformed! But not without the leaven of radical Christianity, which we are called to live out. There is great hope for us—and great hope for the rest of the world through us—if we will come to our knees and repent, return to our God, and recommit ourselves to the righteousness that truly exalts a nation.

2

The Christian Mind Rediscovered

I am much concerned, as I think we all ought to be, about the dumbing down of our culture. This dumbing down is threatening the survival of the Christian mind. The reading interests of Christian people are rapidly diminishing in the areas of theology, ethics, church history, and spiritual formation. We readily use our intellects in our degree occupations—and perhaps even in reading mystery novels or devouring consumer magazines on computer hardware while we sip Original Chai tea and Starbucks coffee over at Barnes and Noble—but not in the serious pursuit of a confessional understanding of our Kingdom calling. God wants us to love him with a spiritual mind in this and in all areas of our lives.

Loving the Lord with all of our mind is part of Christ's great summary of the law in Matthew 22:37, where Jesus says to a lawyer, "You shall love the Lord your God with all your heart, and with all your soul, and with all your mind."[1] In *Knowing Scripture*, R.C. Sproul writes: "The Bible is addressed *primarily* though not *exclusively* to our understanding. That means the mind. This is difficult to communicate to modern Christians who are living in what may be the most anti-intellectual period of Western civilization."[2]

To be sure, intellectual love for God is possible through the parabolic, poetic, cinematic, and dramatic. It can at times be less propositional, less word-heavy in its content, and more imaginative and visual. All such uses of the intellect should be part of our evangelism and worship. But, because God has created human beings with minds, we should lovingly use the whole of our minds.

---

1. This and all Scripture quotations are from the New Revised Standard Version. NRSV *Harper Study Bible* (Grand Rapids: Zondervan, 1991).
2. R.C. Sproul, *Knowing Scripture* (Downers Grove: InterVarsity, 1977), 28.

We owe ourselves, our neighbors, and, above all, God, a Christian mind. Harry Blamires has written for us a classic, first published in 1963, entitled *The Christian Mind*. Practically his opening statement is that "There is no longer a Christian mind"[3]:

> Except over a very narrow field of thinking, chiefly touching questions of strictly personal conduct, we Christians in the modern world accept, for the purpose of mental activity, a frame of reference constructed by the secular mind and a set of criteria reflecting secular evaluations. There is no Christian mind; there is no shared field of discourse. . . .[4]

He continues:

> Christianity is emasculated of its intellectual relevance. . . . [A]t the communal level it is little more than an expression of sentimentalized togetherness. . . . [W]e meet only as worshipping beings . . . not as thinking beings . . . [not] as thinking Christians, over the controversial political, social, and cultural issues.[5]

> [W]e have been . . . taught to view with disfavour any earnest attachment to ideas and ideals such as would bring the heat of theoretical controversy into the arena of practical life.[6]

> [W]e have manufactured a false "charity" of the mind, which never takes a stand, but continually yields ground. It is proper to give way to other people's interests: therefore it is proper to give way to other people's ideas.[7]

> We have become afraid of our own convictions.[8]

In response to this "dumb and dumber" trend in culture, Blamires says, "My claim is that if we did shift our ground, if we set about reconstituting the Christian mind, and began by taking for granted the authoritative, God-given nature of the Christian Faith, and re-establishing in ourselves an unfaltering sense of the objectivity of Christian truth, we should find it an exhilarating procedure."[9]

Rediscovering a Christian mind does not mean lapsing into a dry intellectualism that disconnects the theoretical and practical. In reality, the vision of the intellect and the living of the virtues should

---

3. Harry Blamires, *The Christian Mind* (London: SPCK, 1974), 3.
4. Blamires, *Christian Mind*, 4.
5. Blamires, *Christian Mind*, 16.
6. Blamires, *Christian Mind*, 21.
7. Blamires, *Christian Mind*, 39–40.
8. Blamires, *Christian Mind*, 84.
9. Blamires, *Christian Mind*, 117.

coexist in a fruitful tension, a delicate balance. The two sides come together and are held together in Christ. For the action of the Christian is really Christ's action, flowing out of his mind. We owe it to our neighbors to address the question asked by Colson and Pearcey in their book *How Now Shall We Live?* In it, they take inspiration from Abraham Kuyper:

> We must be men and women who will dare to wrest Christianity free from its fortress mentality, its sanctuary stronghold, and establish it once again as the great life system and cultural force that acknowledges the Creator as sovereign over all. . . . We must be men and women who see, as Kuyper did, that the struggle is one of first principles. "If the battle is to be fought with honor and with a hope of victory, then principle must be arrayed against principle." We must understand opposing views as total life systems and then "take our stand in a life system of equally comprehensive and far-reaching power."[10]

In Romans 12:1–2, Paul writes: "I appeal to you therefore, brothers and sisters, by the mercies of God, to present your bodies as a living sacrifice, holy and acceptable to God, which is your spiritual worship. Do not be conformed to this world, but be transformed by the renewing of your minds, so that you may discern what is the will of God—what is good and acceptable and perfect."

According to verse 2, the key to making the sacrifice of our whole acting selves to God and to living transformed Christian lives is "the renewing of your minds," whereby we prove to God, to ourselves, and to the world what is the good, acceptable, and perfect will of God.

Of course, the tendency for all of us, contrary to verse 1, is to let our minds be conformed to the prevailing spirits of the age, and by our compromising, secular lifestyles prove to God, to ourselves, and to the world that we, aside from our God talk, are no different than any others in this morally blended society where the supreme virtue is tolerance without judgment.

But God wants far more from us. He wants radically holy lives, acceptable to him, even if not acceptable to our contemporaries.

---

10. Charles Colson and Nancy Pearcey, *How Now Shall We Live?* (Wheaton, IL: Tyndale House, 1999), 36.

He wants the transformative power of Christ to be proven in our lives. And all of this has to start with the renewal of our thinking.

In some ways, it is easier to say what the Christian mind is not and identify that to which it stands in negative contrast, than to describe it more positively in its renewed state. Here is a beginning attempt, with much assistance from Blamires. The Christian mind attempts to see everything with transcendence, by borrowing the eyes of God. As the French poet-priest, Michel Quoist, put it in his *Prayers:*

> I would like to rise very high, Lord;
> Above my city,
> Above the world,
> Above time.
> I would like to purify my glance and borrow your eyes.
> I would then see the universe, humanity, history, as the Father sees them.[11]

As another illustration, I include here a piece the LORD gave to me as a vision one Lord's Day. It is entitled *Borrowed Eyes*:

> It was the Lord's Day
> when my thoughts took flight.
>
> And I saw, as it were, a likeness of God.
> There was a huge hand holding a very wide heart.
> The heart was crimson red,
> covered with a thousand translucent eyes,
> like white, emerald and purple sapphires.
> Some turned inward;
> some were in sabbath repose;
> others looked outward in all directions.
>
> And a second hand took me up into its vast strength.
> Its warmth and gentle pressure liquefied me,
> and I was poured into the all-seeing eyes.
>
> Settled deep into the heart of God,
> my sense of body returned,

---

11. Michel Quoist, *Prayers* (Kansas City: Sheed & Ward, 1963), 13–14.

but I felt no desire to stand.
Lying prostrate on the heart's inner face,
and supported by the comfort of His thousand eyes,
I was amazed at what I could see.

The earth came into view,
and upon it appeared a thousand living things.
Each creature stood out with such clarity
that it seemed as though a single eye of God were upon it,
watching it day and night,
magnifying its every instinct or thought,
tracing its every movement,
hearing its distinct cries, however faint,
peering into its face,
even counting the fibers or feathers on its body.

I saw a baby Robin fallen from its nest,
cowering and chirping in fear of an approaching cat.
I saw an adolescent man in his jail cell
throwing up on the cement floor,
sickened by sexual molestation.
I saw a mother and father wailing in a birthing room
over their still-born baby.

I saw into a dark grotto
where a small pot of watery gruel,
supposed to feed a family of twelve,
was cooking over a fire of burning dung.
I saw a man, behind the closed doors of a plush office,
downloading pictures of his favorite fetish.
I saw an aneurysm developing in a mother's brain,
poised in a few minutes to blow its cerebral fuse,
while children stood by helplessly.

For the brief moment of the dream
I thought: All my life
I have seen heaven from earth.
I have worshipped,

> I have adored,
> I have praised.
>
> But now, with borrowed eyes
> and bended gaze,
> my worship is leveled,
> my adoration refracted,
> my praise is returned
> in lament.
>
> It was the Lord's Day
> when my thoughts took flight.
> I saw earth from heaven.
>
> All was changed
> that Day.[12]

To return to Blamires and to quote him once again, the Christian mind is ". . . the view which sets all earthly issues within the context of the eternal, the view which relates all human problems—social, political, cultural—to the doctrinal foundations of the Christian Faith, the view which sees all things here below in terms of God's supremacy and earth's transitoriness. . . ."[13]

Because it has transcendence, the Christian mind is not just swept along by the ever-changing currents of culture. It is honest and bold enough to make "prophetic condemnation of salient features of contemporary secularism."[14] It has "the courage to become relevant by becoming biblical," as David Wells says in *Losing Our Virtue*.[15]

With transcendence rooted in divine revelation, the Christian mind is able to address political, social, educational, cultural issues with a principial, intellectually respectable, biblically informed frame of reference, but "do so in total detachment from any political alignment or prejudice."[16]

---

12. Originally appeared in *Pro Rege* 34, no. 2 (December 2004): 32–33.
13. Blamires, *Christian Mind*, 3–4.
14. Blamires, *Christian Mind*, 8.
15. David Wells, *Losing Our Virtue* (Grand Rapids: Eerdmans, 1998), 199.
16. Blamires, *Christian Mind*, 14.

Political polarization is a severe problem today, and it has almost frozen our Christian voice because we find it so difficult to address any issue except within the typical parameters of political debate.

Democrats are all about using the means of government for responsible *economic* controls, for example, limiting the profits of drug companies; raising the minimum wage; accelerating taxation of the rich to sustain the poor; subsidizing health care, and so on.

Republicans are all about using the means of government for responsible *social* controls, for example, legislation to protect life at its gestational beginning, legislation to protect life at its vulnerable later stages when it becomes meaningless, legislation to place controls on sexual expression and enforce traditional definitions of marriage and family, and so on.

The problem is—and it is the source of severe polarization—Democrats generally do not want social controls, and Republicans do not want economic controls.

The distinction between economic and social controls is one way of describing the ideological polarization today between the political parties. But there are many other ways. I made an attempt at such description in three little pieces, which now follow.

Beginnings of Judgment

Why must we choose between:
exclusive truth and celebration of diversity
reasonable taxation and justice for all
industrial growth and environmental stewardship
states' rights and federal protections
private affairs and the public's right to know
porn-free theaters and smoke-free restaurants
priests and therapists
punishment and rehabilitation
confronting the sin and treating the disease
cutting off and cutting slack
telling the truth and speaking in love
Wall Street projections and unemployment reductions
free markets and fair trade
stay-at-home moms and women working for equal pay

evangelical and ecumenical
hard work and welfare
charity and social security
abstinence and safe sex
headship and egality
law and freedom
victims' rights and offenders' rights
civic responsibilities and civil liberties
pessimism and optimism
realism and idealism
capitalism and socialism
submission and liberation
individual and community
developers and preservationists
unborn and women
conservative and liberal
teaching moral standards and clarifying values
gun rights and animal rights
respect for adults and sensitivity to youth
majorities and minorities
exclusive and inclusive
a cure for cancer and a cure for AIDS
private property and public domain
pay for yourself and pay for others
private physician and socialized medicine
standards of decency and freedom of speech
censorship and liberal arts
the interference clause and the establishment clause?

Why must we choose?
Will we judge rightly if we do?
Will our judgment leave us with half the truth?
Will our spirits become biased and judgmental?
And are the ways of hypocrisy far behind?

The Ways of Hypocrisy

Questions for the left:
Why fight the costs of smoking,

but ignore the costs of drinking?
Why justice for the powerless poor,
but not for the powerless unborn?
Why tolerate the rave
and belittle the religious rally?
Why so much that is relative,
so little absolute?
Why is earth such a pleasure,
but heaven not a longing?
Why excuses for the adulterer,
none for the abuser?
Why the disconnect between unchastity and AIDS,
the connect between smoking and cancer?
Why is right to privacy a defense for abortion,
but privacy of sex so little defended?

Questions for the right:
Why is heaven such a longing,
earth so ignored?
Why are illegals refused bread,
but offered faith?
Why so much black and white,
so little nuance of color?
Why such patriotism,
so little self-critique?
Why blame of employees,
but excuses for management?
Why right to life for the unborn,
not quality of life for the born?
Why does a drop in the stock market
matter more than a rise in health costs?
Why toleration for corporate greed,
but unawareness of global need?
Why becoming rich as a goal,
gaining the world but losing one's soul?

Ah, the ways of hypocrisy!

Peace Psalm

Lord, why do sin-haters
not love sinners more?
Why do sinner-lovers
not hate sin more?
Why cannot law enforcers
become more free with mercy?
Why cannot rights pushers
accept moral limits?
Why cannot Republicans
become more Democratic?
Why cannot Democrats
become more Republican?
Why cannot power abusers
accept greater blame?
Why cannot perpetual victims
accept responsibility for their actions?
Why cannot whites
put on the shoes of blacks?
Why cannot blacks
stop blaming whites?
Why cannot God's chosen
give a home to Ishmael?
Why cannot Muslims
stop scapegoating the Jews?
Why cannot Israelis
bear to pass through Samaria?
Why cannot the Samaritans
worship also on Mt. Zion?
Why cannot free enterprisers
pay a just tax for all?
Why cannot social welfarers
do more themselves for the poor?
Why is big business
so driven by profits?
Why are the tree huggers
so naïve about business?

> Why can't the warriors
> seek more patiently for peace?
> Why can't the peace marchers
> see there's a time for just war?

*"But now in Christ Jesus you who once were far off
have been brought near by the blood of Christ.
For he is our peace:
in his flesh he has made both groups into one
and has broken down the dividing wall,
that is, the hostility between us."* (Ephesians 2:13–14)

> Lord Jesus Christ, have mercy on us.
> Lord Jesus Christ, grant us your peace.

We don't all have to end up thinking entirely alike, for we all have differing personalities and intellectual bents, but neither should we allow ourselves as a Christian community to drift into the same kind of polarization that has come to affect the national political community.

Finally, let me say this: Because the renewed Christian mind is grounded in the transcendent Logos and Love of God, it is able to speak the truth in love, understanding that "There is no charity without clarity and firmness,"[17] and there is no clarity and firmness without charity. In Romans 12:9–19, Paul writes, "Let love be genuine; hate what is evil, hold fast to what is good; love one another with mutual affection; outdo one another in showing honor."

We must find this hate/love balance if we aim to think and speak with a Christian mind. Somehow we have to recover both a righteous anger ("hate what is evil") and an unconditional Christ-empowered compassion ("love one another'), even for those whose beliefs and actions occasion our anger.

Paul says that those who think with renewed Christian minds understand that genuine love is to hate what is evil and hold fast to what is good, while loving with genuine affection those who practice and teach the very evil God calls his people to hate. Can we

---

17. Blamires, *Christian Mind*, 40.

love the radical postmodernist, the relativist, the subjectivist, the humanist while still challenging his/her ideas in the public square? Can we love and serve the homosexual person while still rejecting homosexual behavior? Can we celebrate all persons as precious image bearers of God without having to tolerate silently or even celebrate openly all possible lifestyles, religions, and ideologies? This is the true challenge of our time. And I tell you that it is an overwhelmingly impossible challenge to meet unless one is empowered by the truth and love of Jesus Christ enabling one to say with full conviction: "I can do all things through him who strengthens me" (Philippians 4:13).

There are so many issues today that cry out for the attention and direction of the Christian mind, that cry out for a righteous blend of truth and love. There are so many challenges before us to prove to God, to ourselves, and to the world what is the good, acceptable, and perfect will of God.

I truly believe that we as Christians can work together constructively toward a radically renewed Christian mind and a truly confessional consensus. We can do this because Jesus is our Lord, and he is truth and love; he is the Christian mind incarnate. Only Jesus, by the power of his Spirit, can keep us from "bare conjecture or cold rationalism," but produce instead a transformed "life of vibrant passion" by the renewal of our minds and the empowerment of our love.

3

Christianity in Culture: Three Paths

The most fundamental thing that can be said about human beings is that they are religious beings whose existence flows out of their relationship as creatures to their Creator. Religion, from the Latin *religere*, meaning "to bind back or together," is a word describing our inescapable relationship with our Creator God. We are creatures bound back to God, inescapably religious. God continues to reveal himself, and we continue to respond, in one way or another. Our response flows from our hearts to permeate and determine in a totalitarian way every other aspect of our existence. Henry R. Van Til puts it this way in *The Calvinistic Concept of Culture:* "No man can escape this religious determination of his life, since God is the inescapable, ever-present *Fact* of man's existence. God may be loved or hated, adored or debased, but he cannot be ignored. The sense of God (*sensus deitatis*) is still the seed of religion (*semen religionis*)."[1]

Religion comes to expression in *cultura* and *cultus*. They are the two streams that flow out of our religious experience.

Culture comes to expression in our re-creation, re-production, and artistic re-formation of creation as we willfully exercise our God-given dominion over the earth. Culture links up with work (*labora*), perspiration, and deeds of service, but also with leisure, which is the freedom to be in school, to be taught and to learn the liberal arts, and the freedom to be at play and to experience a change of pace (sabbath) in the midst of life's endeavors. Work and leisure are seen by Josef Pieper in his book *Leisure: The Basis of Culture* as "twin expressions" of "the articulation of a joint, so that the one is hardly intelligible without the other."[2]

---

1. Henry R. Van Til, *The Calvinistic Concept of Culture* (Grand Rapids: Baker, 2001), 37–38.
2. Josef Pieper, *Leisure: The Basis of Culture* (New York: Random House, 1963), 21–22.

Cultus is the expression of religion in worship, prayer *(ora)*, aspiration. When linked with the ritual of sacrifice, worship is something people do in the separate organizational sphere of the Church. However, in a broader sense, the expression of religion as worship reveals itself in the Church as organism and thus informs everything that people do in their work and leisure culture-creating activity.

What I really want to get at in talking about all this is the issue of how we as Christians can bring our religion to expression in our culture and cultus. H. Richard Niebuhr, in his significant book *Christ and Culture,* lays out the three basic paths that Christians have tried to follow. They are *accommodation, separation,* and *transformation.*[3]

Accommodation, the way of compromise and contextualization, gradually becomes conformity and ultimately deformation. Not a good path to go. The second path, separation, is a path of retreat. It is a survival tactic. Survival is sought by significant withdrawal from the world, so as not to be of it, so as not to be consumed by it. Roles in government and in other secular institutions are largely avoided as Christians build their own societies. The problem here can become a minimalization of Christian influence and compartmentalization of life into spiritual and secular.

I, as a Protestant Christian, am part of the Reformed tradition that traces its roots back to John Calvin. Of the three paths described by Niebuhr, we Reformed thinkers prefer the path of transformation. Using the model of Abraham Kuyper's "every square inch" philosophy, we believe that Christ is Lord of the universe and that as we interact with the various religious forces that are creating culture, we deliberately seek to penetrate and transform. We try to stay in the world so as to redeem it, even while we try not to be of it—to avoid conformity—and try not to withdraw from it.

However, transformation is no small challenge. It is fraught with perils. The principalities and powers and world rulers of this present darkness link themselves with various cultural expressions and produce powerful momentums that work against the principles of the kingdom of God. I call these momentums the *ethoi* or spirits of an age, which may be referred to as "the culture" in the broader sense. They may assume such names as Western culture or Islamic

---

3. H. Richard Niebuhr, *Christ and Culture* (New York: Harper, 1951).

culture, for example. Various *-isms* rise to the surface in such cultures. In Western culture, they are such ideologies as individualism, privatism, hedonism, materialism, consumerism, subjectivism, and so on. The ethoi or spirits can also be identified as various trends of *praxis* or behavior. Four examples come immediately to mind: the theater and entertainment industry, the gaming industry (poker and gambling), the competitive sports culture, the computer/Internet culture. Many others could be mentioned.

Thorough-going Reformed folk say to themselves: We must redeem these activities, these entertainments, these technologies, these sports. We must seize them back from the enemy and put them under the control of our Lord Jesus Christ. And in that, we are absolutely right. We can't simply write off segments of our existence and say that these are secular territories we dare not lay claim to or that these square inches are off limits.

But how do we do that? What is our strategy? Some would say that we need to send people into the Hollywood ranks to infiltrate and leaven. Or we can safely sponsor church poker tournaments because we will simply eliminate the gambling. Or we can safely and enthusiastically enter the sports arena and attempt to nurture a sports culture radically different than the highly competitive, money-driven, win-at-all-costs, steroid-using, prima-donna culture that has developed. We need not discard our computers and shut off our e-mails and discontinue the Internet because we will not be tempted to abuse and addiction. Rather, we must remind ourselves occasionally that this is cultural terrain where we can and must tread, because if we don't stay in the arena, how can we hope to transform it? We seem to have this naïve trust in ourselves that we surely will make responsible use of our liberties.

Our transforming ideals are noble. But what generally happens in the arts, in business, in our uses of computer technology, in our sports and recreations, in our discernments regarding theater and movie entertainments, and so on? We gradually become assimilated into the cultural mainstream, swept along by the tastes, movements, powers and practices of everyone else in the world around us. Our devotion to Christian liberty, our annoyance with accountability within the believing community, and our fear of censure and persecution by the world leave us powerless and compromised.

We do little, with some notable exceptions, to transform our culture because we have already bought into it so significantly. It transforms us by luring us into conformity, and the upshot is moral decline, ethical reductionism, and, tragically, spiritual deformation.

The momentums of culture, driven by the principalities and powers, are leading us around. We are not the pacesetters of culture we should be. The Church today is powerless and compromised. There is little ethical radicality left in its message. The ring is in its nose. Many Christian institutions (like schools and colleges) are fast losing their distinctiveness and becoming spiritually and morally generic. Visions of practical holiness are diminishing as the driving force at these institutions.

On a broader front, such forces as personal rights fulfillment, egalitarianism, and materialism are leading us into paths destructive of the family and of marriage. The acquisition of things, of property and wealth, the pursuit of personal pleasures, and the deification of careers at the expense of children shuffled off to day-care centers are all negative momentums of culture against which we as Christians are demonstrating less and less power to resist. The world is shaping more and more of the cultural square yards and miles, not to mention inches, that are occupied by Christians committed to transformity.

Historically, some Christians, like the Anabaptists, Mennonites, Amish, and certain Methodists, have said that we must therefore take the path of separatism. We must set up legalistic standards and barriers that isolate and insulate us from the destructive forces of the world. We must cluster up into our own colonies and basically withdraw from the rat race.

In the case of the Amish, the style of separation becomes extreme and ends up blocking off entire segments of culture because of the inherent dangers seen to be implicit in them—whether it be electricity, the automobile, gasoline tractors, or whatever.

But maybe we should think more about this. Maybe the answer doesn't lie entirely in either the transformational or the separationist models of being Christians in the world. Maybe a return to Scripture, the Old and New Testaments, would cause us to reconsider a kind of combination model of separation and transformation.

What do I mean? Well, think for a moment of the Kingdom/ mission strategy of God for his people in the Old Testament dispensation. The same God who gave his people a cultural mandate also called them to come out and be separate. The mission vision was centripetal, meant to draw other nations in by the radical holiness of the lives and worship of God's people structuring their lives around the law of God. The hope was that the surrounding peoples would take hold of the skirts of the Jewish believers and come with them to Zion. The compelling draw, the magnet, would be the holiness of God's people. And this is what would be transforming. This is what would fulfill God's ultimate purpose for the election of his set-apart people; Israel was not chosen unto privilege, suspicion, hubris, fear and judgment, but unto a compelling mission of drawing others into the kingdom of God. This, in turn, becomes the backdrop for the Great Commission to Christians in the New Testament, which is to "Go." The vision becomes centrifugal, moving from the center outward.

But is the Christian vision exclusively centrifugal? Is the desert entirely left behind? Is there not a prior calling out of the Church, the *ecclesia*, before it is sent out? Does not transformation still need a spiritual formation foundation? Does not the centripetal continue to give basis to the centrifugal? Is there not a continuing election strategy involving the *selecting out* of the twelve apostles, which puts them in close company with Jesus the Master Discipler for three and a half years but which does not thereby imply the *rejection* of just about everyone else? Rather, it is a withdrawal and in-depth training of a few so that they might not only magnetically draw the Gentiles in, but actively go out to them because the Kingdom of Christ is directed intentionally to all peoples and even to the entire earth. In other words, the goal is transformation: the full realization of the Kingdom of God, a kingdom of righteousness and holiness. But the continuing strategy of relevance is separation.

To do mission effectively in the cultural wasteland of our contemporary setting, we have to withdraw to a radically-different kind of God-occupied desert, which we find to be our fruitful origination point for resurrected ministry. And though this desert of retreat may seem to be even more barren and solitary than the cultural desert, the devotional/literary testimonies of biblical characters and other saints who have dared to step back and go there, tell us that this desert is a place where life germinates anew beneath the sand.

It is a place where the whisper of God's voice is rediscovered, as he speaks out of some arid breeze, or prickly cactus, or dry waterbed.

Jesus began his journey into the wasteland of a God-starved world by first retreating to God's desert. The devil was there to tempt Jesus, but it was a God-occupied place, nevertheless. In God's wilderness of solitude, Jesus responded to the enticements of pleasure, fame, and power with absolute trust in the sufficiency of the quoted Word of God not to return void, but to accomplish that to which it was sent.

And so must we, like Jesus, stand first in that same place of solitude if we hope to fulfill our desert mission in the world for Christ's sake.

In a very real sense, Jesus remained a desert-seeker throughout his whole public ministry. It seemed that he remained a stranger to the big cities, the urban, sophisticated, fast-paced life of the affluent and well-educated. Jesus kept resisting the disciples' urgings to capture the momentum of crowd interest, as for example in Capernaum. He called his disciples instead to follow him to the *komopoleis,* the hick-towns and dusty out-of-the-way places (see Mark 1:36-38). T. S. Eliot recognized in Jesus this identity of the "Stranger" returning always to the desert after challenging the city about its empty, hollow values, saying:

> Though you have shelters and institutions,
> Precarious lodgings while the rent is paid,
> Subsiding basements where the rat breeds
> Or sanitary dwellings with numbered doors
> Or a house a little better than your neighbour's;
> When the Stranger says: "What is the meaning of this city?
> Do you huddle close together because you love each other?"
> What will you answer? "We all dwell together
> To make money from each other?" or "This is a community"?
> And the Stranger will depart and return to the desert.
> O my soul, be prepared for the coming of the Stranger,
> Be prepared for Him who knows how to ask questions.[4]

Later, in the same poem, Eliot described how Jesus, the desert seeker, viewed the ideal Church: not as a great successful institution

---

4. T. S. Eliot, "Choruses from 'The Rock,'" *The Complete Poems and Plays: 1909–1950* (New York: Harcourt, Brace, and World, 1952), 103.

aligned with the state and living in comfortable accommodation with its culture, but as a humble body of martyrs and saints who would build God's temple the right way—with their convictions and their blood:

> Why should men love the Church? Why should they love her laws?
> She tells them of Life and Death, and of all that they would forget.
> She is tender where they would be hard, and hard where they like to be soft.
> She tells them of Evil and Sin, and other unpleasant facts.
> They constantly try to escape
> From the darkness outside and within
> By dreaming of systems so perfect that no one will need to be good.
> But the man that is will shadow
> The man that pretends to be.
> And the Son of Man was not crucified once for all,
> The blood of martyrs not shed once for all,
> The lives of the Saints not given once for all:
> But the Son of Man is crucified always
> And there shall be Martyrs and Saints.
> And if blood of Martyrs is to flow on the steps
> We must first build the steps;
> And if the Temple is to be cast down
> We must first build the Temple.[5]

Such manner of building the Temple (of growing the Church) is a forbidding course and none but the saints and martyrs will want to follow. In the truest sense, it is a desert trail, not a wide superhighway of success, of gladisms and be-happy-attitudes.

Growing the Church by investing deeply in just a few disciples who come to understand that the call of Christ is something to be lived out in depth and in death seems an old-fashioned strategy in a media-driven, entertainment-oriented, happiness-hungry culture. And so there are the worship/music wars and style conflicts and the debates about re-formation of ethics and evangelism so as to grow the Church. And if the responsible path is chosen through this thicket of potential compromises, it turns out to be costly. There is much dying taking place on the narrow trail of obedience to biblical authority and evangelism.

We can stay on the road of desert mission for Jesus' sake if we are ready to follow the narrow way of radical discipleship. Minority

---

5. *Ibid.*, p. 106.

trends on the narrow way have been set by the lives of the prophets, the apostles, and the saints of the Church, some of whom were literal desert fathers and mothers, but all of whom were desert dwellers in the sense that they all took the path less traveled.

Sometimes in its history the Church has slipped over to the road more traveled. Back in the fourth century after Christ, the Christian Church was experiencing a time of tremendous numerical growth. Since Emperor Theodosius had issued an edict in 381 declaring Christianity to be the official religion of the Roman Empire, everyone, it seemed, wanted to be baptized. Obviously, for many, faith became very superficial and nominal, and the Church came under serious spiritual threat. This at a time when the growth in numbers was astounding!

Soon renewal movements began to appear. People like John Cassian, a young student in Rome, went to join spiritual leaders like the Desert Fathers in Egypt. Monasticism was on the rise. Little communities of faith came together to preserve the scriptures, to read, recite, and pray the Word of God. Collective memories of Scripture were shared and prayed during the offices of the day.

Eventually some of these faith communities developed into more formal religious orders like the Benedictines under the Rule written by Benedict of Nursia. In these religious communities, sincere Christian men and women were able to keep their spirits alive and preserve the spiritual disciplines of reading, studying, memorizing, meditating on and praying the scriptures, as well as using silence, solitude, fasting, simplicity, and chastity as reinforcements.

The minority monastic movement itself came under temptations and compromises. The devil is active on any trail, however out-of-the-way or untraveled it may be. But God has often, through the history of the Church, used the withdrawals of Christians to preserve the holy mission of the Church. Aggressive promotion of church growth, associated as it sometimes is with latching on to the momentums of the time, is not necessarily an advance of the kingdom of God. Often real advances have been made through strategic retreats.

The life of Patrick, missionary to the Irish in the fifth century A.D., as told by Charles Colson in *How Now Shall We Live*, is a powerful testimony of kingdom advancement through withdrawal. Here are a few excerpts from a much longer account:

> St. Patrick brought the Christian message of love and forgiveness and established monasteries throughout the land. The monastic movement in Ireland began to revolutionize the world, replacing the old values of a warrior society with the new values of Christianity. . . . eventually a flood of missionaries from Ireland fanned out across Scotland, England, and the European continent. All along the way the monks established monasteries and carried on their tradition of copying and preserving the bible, along with every other book they could get their hands on—including the great classics of the Greeks and Romans. . . . it was the disciplined labor of the monks that stanched the tide of barbarism across Europe, preserved the best of Greco-Roman culture, and infused new life into the decadent monasticism of the continent. The monastery became the center of culture, replacing the dying cities and expanding into a vast complex populated by monks, workers, servants, and dependents. . . . As the barbarians were converted and the destructive invasions ceased, European society began to flourish. Cities grew, guilds emerged to protect the interests of the crafts and professions, and ideas of representative government took root.
>
> In this setting, Christianity gave birth to a new institution, the university, which developed from schools attached to the great cathedrals in places such as Paris and Bologna, eventually replacing the monasteries as centers of learning and culture.[6]

As modern day universities have almost completely distanced themselves from their roots, new forces of philosophical and moral barbarism with a modern face have established themselves in the very centers of learning and culture intended to liberate us from such forces. Social change through spiritual reform is needed. But perhaps the way will once again be withdrawal into the desert by those who still acknowledge Christ as Lord. Perhaps we should even begin to question whether only university-educated teachers, with doctoral certifications from state-supported institutions that have totally embraced secular humanism as their exclusive religion of choice, should be our instructors in Christian colleges and even seminaries.

---

6. Charles Colson and Nancy Pearcey, *How Now Shall We Live?* (Wheaton: Tyndale House, 1999), 300–302.

I think we can see from the example of Patrick that the Church is not just its own cultic institution to which kingdom-building Christians in their cultural endeavors now and then retreat (whether that be to a monastery or to a church sanctuary). It does have an organizational expression, but it is also a model of holiness-living that trains and calls us to pursue separateness, distinctness, and Christlikeness in our daily cultural mandate-fulfilling activities as the Church organism in various spheres.

Only holiness can attract. Only holiness can transform. Transformation built on a foundation of conformity is as powerless as an empty word. And transformation, to be really effective, requires community. And community, in turn, requires accountability and mutual responsibility.

We must pray that we may truly become the people of God in our separate churches and institutions, not just temporary collections of Christian individuals fractionalized by our fascination with personal freedoms. To paraphrase Paul, we must become subject to, and servants of, one another out of reverence for Christ. We must not, as the Gentiles of this present secular culture, abandon ourselves to licentiousness. We are called to put away our former manner of life, our old selves, and to be renewed in the spirit of our minds. We are called to put on the clothing of the new self, created according to the likeness of God in true righteousness and holiness.

St. Paul expresses our commission succinctly in these words:

> Now this I affirm and insist on in the Lord: you must no longer live as the Gentiles live, in the futility of their minds. They are darkened in their understanding, alienated from the life of God, because of their ignorance and hardness of heart. They have lost all sensitivity and have abandoned themselves to licentiousness, greedy to practice every kind of impurity. That is not the way you learned Christ! For surely you have heard about him and were taught in him, as truth is in Jesus. You were taught to put away your former way of life, your old self, corrupt and deluded by its lusts, and to be renewed in the spirit of your minds, and to clothe yourselves with the new self, created according to the likeness of God in true righteousness and holiness. (Ephesians 4:17–24)

4

Postmodernist Culture and the Christian Mind

Societal pulse-takers are telling us that we have definitely moved past a modern into a postmodern consciousness. The prevailing worldview appears to include some of the following, as gleaned from the writings of people such as Francis Foucault, Jacques Derrida, Stanley Fish, and Richard Rorty.

1. There is no objective view of reality. Each person constructs his/her own view. Nor is there a normative, transcendent worldview (such as the rational meta-narrative of the Enlightenment), only many self-validating views, each with their own temporal validity. David F. Wells, in his book, *Above All Earthly Pow'rs: Christ in a Postmodern World,* illustrates this view from the writings of Richard Rorty, who, says Wells,

> ... rejects every claim to having meaning or truth which has some particular starting premise at the foundation and a structure built upon it by some method of inference. The mind, he contends, does not reflect the world "out there" as a mirror might, and he also rejects the view that language is capable of describing what is there. There is, therefore, no position that one can find that is outside of life from which to make "objective" judgments which represent what is there. In the end, "truth" becomes relative to the person for whom it is true.[1]

2. Our assertions, our stories, our descriptions about what is true and good need not correspond to some objective truth or good out there. They may be true and good for us, for this time, but not necessarily for other people or other times. Here is how Wells describes it:

---

1. David F. Wells, *Above All Earthly Pow'rs* (Grand Rapids: Eerdmans, 2006), 81.

This postmodern outlook comes in all kinds of shapes and expression, which is what probably explains the multiplicity of definitions which have been advanced. Its own ethos almost guarantees that there will be no such thing as *a* postmodern outlook but rather there will be many different postmodern perspectives. Yet what they have in common is that they all believe that meaning has died. . . .

. . . all thought is conditioned by its cultural context and must, accordingly, be acknowledged as being relative. . . .

What has replaced the worldviews that once sought to encompass the whole of existence in their understanding are now privatized worldviews, worldviews that are valid for no one but the person whose world it is and whose view it is.[2]

3. Our ethical values, then, are only that—relative values—reflecting subjective judgments about rights and wrongs, not based in moral absolutes giving them lasting normativity. In Wells's words again: "values replace virtues, personality replaces character, and the self takes the place that human nature had once had."[3]

We may wonder why or how such a postmodern view has emerged. Is it possible that intellectuals like Foucault, Derrida, Fish, and Rorty have had such influence outside the academy as to affect the thoughts and habits of millions of people in the Western world? I appreciate the insight that David Wells brings to this question. He sees a link between postmodern culture and consumer culture. These are his words, quoted extensively:

Why, one wonders, has the canopy of meaning collapsed so completely on so many? It strains credulity . . . that this is the consequence of individuals' having read the work of intellectuals like Foucault and Derrida. I am, therefore, much more inclined to look for explanations, partial though they may be, in the experience of living in this highly urbanized and consumption-driven culture. What, in particular, might have pushed people to these positions?

. . . what we need to understand is how our society is now dominated by consumer appetite. And it is in the set of attitudes that emerge from within the consumer that we find some of the causes for the breakdown of our ability to sustain a worldview larger than our own individual existence. And the key here is the myriad of choices with which consumers are confronted every day. . . .

---

2. Wells, *Above All Earthly Pow'rs*, 67, 74.
3. Wells, *Above All Earthly Pow'rs*, 58.

In fact, in America anything and everything can be "commodified" and sold, from style to sex, from ideas to religion. . . . This is Western freedom and Western commercialized culture. Here, we have the ability to hope for what we want, shop where we want, buy what we want, study where we want, think what we want, believe what we want, and treat religion as just another commodity, a product to be consumed.

The reality is that modern consumption is not simply about shopping because what we are buying is not simply goods and services. Modern consumption is about buying *meaning* for ourselves. It is about the way we construct ourselves, the vantage point from which we want to look at the world. It is, therefore, becoming the defining focus of a new kind of civilization. What was once just a matter of producing goods has become a way of producing culture and meaning. . . .

It is quite striking, then, to note the parallels between postmodern habits of mind and the realities which have come to mark our highly formed capitalism: volatility, obsolescence, the rapid passing of fashions and ideas, the disappearance of stability, constant innovation, constant revision, repackaging, the new look, the newer than new product, the future always looming over the present.[4]

The cultural shift to postmodernism is not without significant consequence. I cite five things:

a. With the death of the Enlightenment, belief in inevitable progress, confidence in some ultimate purpose or destiny collapses also. Life becomes all about ". . . our habits of consumption. We move as nomads from one oasis to another, ever shopping and never stopping, defining ourselves only by what is present and by what can be purchased and experienced."[5]

b. Since truth and morality are subjective, consensus is not possible. The quest for philosophical unity is futile. With the emergence of tolerance as the supreme virtue, serious discussion of ideas and issues becomes tedious—just a language game. Debate polarizes.

c. Postmodern media emphasis shifts from content to package, from truth to style. Emotive effect, practical usefulness for the moment, sensual appeal, and reality-show voyeurism—these things become the predominant focus.

d. In religious circles affected by postmodernism, creeds become cumbersome ballast; commitments are cast off; moral mandates

---

4. Wells, *Above All Earthly Pow'rs*, 75–77.
5. Wells, *Above All Earthly Pow'rs*, 89.

become personal, purpose-driven prerogatives. The be-happy-attitudes replace the Beatitudes. Spirituality is still pursued, but at the expense of laying every ethical weight aside. The wave of popular tastes in music, entertainments, and life styles threatens to capsize the boat of moral stability and leave the Church awash in a sea of pop culture.

e. In the study of literature, the operative word becomes *deconstructionism*, meaning that literature is empty of meaning; all truths are merely opinions, influenced by social and historical context. A new post-modern hermeneutics governs the approach to all original texts, whether they be Plato's *Republic*, Calvin's *Institutes*, Shakespeare's plays, Donne's metaphysical poetry, *The U.S. Constitution*, or, yes, even the Bible itself.

For illustration, let's do a playful exercise in postmodern hermeneutics. The word *hermeneutics*, incidentally, refers to the science of interpreting written texts, especially the Bible, and originates in the name *Hermes*, the ancient Greek messenger of the gods.

An Old, Old Story

Jack and Jill went up the hill
to fetch a pail of water.
Jack fell down and broke his crown,
and Jill came tumbling after.

Newer Versions

Tyler and Taylor
went jogging together,
slurping their bottled water.
Taylor fell down,
just fooling around!
And Tyler came tumbling after.

Matthew and Megan
skied down the hill
to fetch their Perrier water.
Matthew drank first
and quenched his thirst.
Megan drank thereafter.

Austin and Ashley
sauntered through the valley
to find some spring-fed water.
Austin fell down
and bruised his crown,
so Ashley went after the water.

Both Beth and Zach
loved to backpack
and kayak the rapid white water.
But if they rolled over,
Beth always took over,
and Zack was safe thereafter.

Sarah and Hannah explored the savannah and camped near the rustling water.	They both laid down and slept around. Boredom followed after.

Why Newer Is Better

1. Currently, the newer names are among the ten most popular. Why would anybody name their child Jack or Jill?

2. The newer versions of the old story are far less violent. It isn't pleasant to read about someone breaking his crown.

3. Life should not be portrayed as an uphill struggle. Language of jogging, snowboarding, downhill skiing, kayaking, and exploring are much more appealing to the "catch the big wave" tsunami generation.

4. Jack and Jill are still doing chores! But life isn't about working or duty. It's about partying and having fun, about celebrating in happy church, about going crazy in the sports stadium, about hanging out with new friends in the Internet chat room.

5. Grandmother fetched water in a pail. Today, everyone buys it spring-fed and bottled.

6. Jack is far too prominent in the original version. Okay, he falls. But his part in the story is so dramatic, and Jill just comes tumbling after. Better to have the boy be the bumbling idiot, stumbling over the girl who seems never to fall, who finds the water, who brings the kayak under control, who has the good manners to let Jack drink first.

7. Perhaps the best story version is to use genderless language and have both boy and girl be the same in every way (who can distinguish male or female between Taylor and Tyler?), even if it turns out to be boring?

8. Maybe it would be more interesting if the story were about two girls or two boys.

9. Anyway, who can say that making love in a savannah with one's significant other is boring? Better than same-old sex with one's lifelong heterosexual marriage partner!

10. If the language of the Jack and Jill story doesn't fit my postmodern image of myself, then why not blend in my own story with it? This makes better sense of things and rids me of an enormous amount of emotional baggage.

11. The newer versions don't corrupt the original story. They take the corruption out of the old story and are in the end a truer telling. Changing the language doesn't really change the story. Just the names and a few other cultural details have been changed, to protect the innocent . . . listener from being bombarded by abstract and threatening words. And, after all, water is water. Only the containers and the means of securing and enjoying it change. Styles of life change. But the essential story is the same. Besides, the original is, after all, a narrative, not an objective, static truth. It can be reframed by other stories, as long as what remains when the reconstructing is done affirms one's own contemporary experience.

Well, the old Jack and Jill story is one harmless thing; the biblical story is quite another. May we deconstruct it? Is Scripture, like any literary work, empty of fixed and objective meaning, such that its language makes no unchanging disclosure?

If our preferred lifestyles and liberties begin to feel the pinch of biblical norms and laws, may we then reconstruct the story, the truths, the morals so as to fit better with our contemporary conscience?

For example, on the level of social morality:

1. If radical tolerance is the spirit of the age, may we, affected by that spirit, dismiss the teaching of Paul on homosexuality in Romans 1 as but his culturally conditioned views, good for his time but not any longer for our own?

2. May we take the teaching of Paul in Galatians 3:28, about there being neither male nor female when it comes to baptized membership in the body of Christ, and go on imaginatively to draw the further implication that issues of gender distinction are irrelevant in our understanding of legitimate sexual relationships and behavior and our definitions of marriage and the family?

On the level of Christian theology:

1. In the postmodern view, the cross of Christ is not about substitutionary atonement; it is about the example of sacrificial love. Are words like *sin, guilt, justification, regeneration, damnation, judgment,* and *salvation* to disappear from our vocabulary, while new vocabularies of faith emerge, with words like *reconciliation, celebration of diversity,* and *toleration* now predominating the religious discourse?

2. Are we to begin to question also the virgin birth, the incarnation, the resurrection, the notion of heaven and hell, and the trinity—especially the miraculous or supernatural dimension of these stories?

What are we, called to ministry in Christ's name, to do? Do we set aside the weights of creed and commitment so we can travel light in our witness and worship? Do we abandon the language of morality and adopt the vocabulary of therapy? Do we surrender the notion of external authority and find new ways to blend our teachings of the Kingdom of God with the new gospel narratives of the collective self articulated for us, of course, by contemporary communitarian scholars? Do we join those Christian preachers and leaders who are simply avoiding the great questions, urging tolerance, while they problem-solve immediate issues related to human wants? Do we become more entertaining, more sensate, less intellectual? Do we surrender a Christian mind? Do we fine-tune our language and methods of evangelism to the short-term memory, sound-bite learning habits of our thought-challenged contemporaries? Worse yet, do we deconstruct our stories, doctrines, and ethics to fit our contemporary lifestyles?

In the Introduction to his book *The End of the Modern World*, Romano Guardini writes: ". . . the spirit of an age becomes wholly clear only when it has begun to vanish from the face of the earth."[1] Certainly this is no time for us to catch the waning wave of postmodern culture.

Charles Colson wrote in *Against the Night:* "When the church transcends culture, it can transform culture."[2] "Transformation comes about by the renewal, the change of mind (*metanoia*) that is experienced in repentance."[3]

The time has come to call urgently for the regeneration of the Christian mind. Christian leaders need to become, says David Wells, "cognitive dissidents" within culture rather than "amicable partners" with the world.[4] Ministers need to rediscover and entrust

---

1. Romano Guardini, *The End of the Modern World* (Wilmington, DE: Intercollegiate Studies Institute, 1998), xxv.
2. Charles Colson, *Against the Night* (Ann Arbor: Servant, 1989), 137.
3. Colson, *Against the Night,* 140.
4. David F. Wells, *No Place for Truth* (Grand Rapids: Eerdmans, 1993), 136.

themselves to the power of truth, placing less confidence in themselves as professionals managing by technique and relying on mass-communication technologies and feel-good strategies. Proclamation of the Gospel needs to become more submissive to the biblical text, less situational and therapeutic. We need to resist the dumbing down of the Church in message and worship. Most of all, we need to resist the postmodern consciousness and return to obedient Christianity.

If the old, old story of the Gospel were not a story originating from God himself, but merely the religious ruminations of human writers about God, I'd be more inclined to say: Let the story evolve! If Scripture is inspired, but not in any way differently inspired than any other great literary text, then it is, in fact, like theology itself, just speech *about* God! And then why not progress into speech about speech about God? And why not speech about speech about speech about God? Then what does it matter if the names and places, the truths and the values of the Gospel change? What does it matter if there ever really was a moment in history when creation by God *ex nihilo* occurred, when historical events of incarnation or resurrection of the Christ occurred?

But then, what does God finally become? A mere projection of our religious hopes? Does he finally become as fictional as Jack and Jill, but still somehow necessary for our imaginative framing of our own stories?

I am not prepared to go there personally. I believe that we owe God respect, the respect to yield ourselves to his thereness as a personal, self-existent God and to his divine revelation as a story to be received in all its disturbing, comforting, agony-and-hope-producing originality! We need to receive it as a wonderful story of redemption to be celebrated, not recalibrated. And then let us journal and live out our own stories within that story, by way of trusting submission, repentance, and commitment, as we are lost in wonder, awe, and praise for the incredible old story and the ancient storyteller himself, even our sovereign God and Savior who is the same yesterday, today, and always and is blessed forever!

5

Christianity and Secular Humanism

If I could borrow the eyes of God and look through them at the university, my hunch is that I would see this great institution with the glint of a smile reflected through a prism of tears.

God is immensely pleased, I believe, to see so many thousands of people expressing his divine image by using their intellects in creative ways. I feel overwhelmed with a sense of wonder when I consider the incredible capacity of the human mind to invent, to develop, to subdue the elements of creation and make them serve humanity in marvelous ways. Much of this creativity is generated, sustained, and improved in that immensely powerful citadel of learning called the university. Since God is the most creative of all beings, the ultimate Creator, he must be pleased to see his children reflecting back that creativity.

But God also has a tear in his eye as he views the university. In fact, the view must be so painful to him that he must almost be constrained to look away. For in this place, which was originally centered around God and his revelation and where theology was the queen of sciences, God has been removed from the curriculum. Theology is in disarray, in total retreat, at universities today. Only a small minority of universities still require students to take at least one course in philosophy, not to mention religion and ethics.

Whereas universities once pursued holistic, integrated objectives and looked to Christianity to supply this holistic, integrated vision, today universities are becoming mere knowledge factories and specialized training centers. The only unifying factor, according to David Gill, in a speech at the University of Wisconsin, is "the dominance of technique." Religion, if it has any place at all, is compartmentalized and treated as peripheral. Students who graduate from universities emerge with intellectual powers but without holistic wisdom and character; they emerge "armed with doctoral skills and a kindergarten world view," to quote Gill's speech again.

In the following poem, I picture the situation at the typical university today:

Tower of Learning

Scuttling about like the work-ants
and shouldering burdens of books,
students now follow old trailways,
by precedent culturally worn,
to shrines of fine arts and of science.
philosophy, math, and the law,
and drink there from bloodless grails.

The rigors of lectures and schedules,
exams, professorial pressures,
supply the osmosis solution
that gives to these tasks some intention.

Skyscraping factories of knowledge
arise like top-heavy anthills,
like pyramids upside-down,
pedantic mushroom nimbi,
o'erfilled with debris of data
arising from little reasonings—
invisible atom splittings—
to rival the height of Babel
and push out the lordly hosts.

To what end or higher purpose
this Hydra of fact upon fact?
Times past, the mandate from Temple
was merely to point and to praise,
to bow to the sovereign heavens.

Now scholars in guilds of attainment
build miles of microfilm files

> and labs to compute and do research,
> thus forcing the heavens colossal
> into humans' so very small heads,
> neglecting the sacredmost altar
> where all knees should humbly be led.
>
> Wise ants build their homes in the anthill,
> communities by their will, and
> with feet set in soil of the real earth,
> lift their heads to the highest heavens
> like even the poets do still.

God's hurt for the campus, his view of the university scene, is acquainted with grief, I believe, because God has been put on the shelf as irrelevant and also because another competing worldview has come to predominate in the university. It is the worldview of secular humanism. The presence of that prevailing worldview across all of the departments of study is what enables the university to continue as a *uni*versity rather than a *multi*versity, as it has sometimes been mistakenly called because of its extensive specialization.

And what must truly grieve the heart of God is that so many Christian students (and even faculty) come to the university and show little awareness of *antithesis*. They do not seem to understand that secular humanism is a worldview in direct competition with the Christian worldview.

Superficially, it would seem that humanism is a worldview that shares many common goals with Christianity. It would seem that humanists seek to achieve basically the same improvement of the quality of life on earth as socially conscious, sensitive Christians seek. Christians may also aspire to an afterlife in heaven that humanists reject, but as far as the betterment of this world is concerned, both sides are saying many of the same things. Or so it would seem. Thus, many Christians going through the university do so with little sense of what a place of struggle this is—or ought to be.

A closer look reveals the true picture. The worldview of humanism, as summarized contemporarily in the 1933 humanist *Manifesto I* and in the 1973 humanist *Manifesto II*, and the worldview of Christianity, as set forth in Old and New Testament scriptures, are essentially antithetical, except for some very superficial agreements.

Several areas of superficial agreement covering over profound disagreement could be cited. For example, Christians would applaud the idea that religion, in its search for abiding values, remains "an inseparable feature of human life." But when we learn in *Manifesto I* that humanists consider *theistic* religion as outmoded and ready to be replaced by the fifteen affirmations of the new self-proclaimed *religious* humanism that follows, we sense immediately that the battle is joined.

Christians would certainly share the social passion of humanists and seek to express religious emotions "in a heightened sense of personal life and in a cooperative effort to promote social well-being." Christians and humanists are agreed that the sacred and secular cannot be absolutely separated and that people's religious activity includes labor, art, law, science, philosophy, education, recreation, politics, and so on. But Christians would reject the this-world-ism of humanism, which views humankind as simply a product of nature and religious culture as a product of natural environment. They would reject the idea that social heritage, worship, and prayers are humanly insignificant and that belief in the supernatural and the afterlife are inhibitive to the realization of human personality and happiness in this life.

Again, Christians are as convinced as humanists that "existing acquisitive and profit-motivated society has shown itself to be inadequate." However, the answer is not a mere exchange of economic philosophies, a discarding of capitalism for "a socialized and cooperative order." Neither socialistic nor capitalistic ideology capture the truth taught in Scripture. But does Scripture receive any serious attention in the economics departments of contemporary universities?

The issue of the value of human life is another area of superficial agreement. When humanists say in their *Manifesto II* that "The preciousness and dignity of the individual person is a central humanist value," Christians applaud. But the applause turns quickly into disapproval when dignity is then associated with maximum individual autonomy, including the right to abortion, divorce, many varieties of sexual exploration, euthanasia, and suicide. Subsequent statements in *Manifesto II* to the effect that "We are concerned for the welfare of the aged, the infirm, the disadvantaged, and also for the outcasts—the mentally retarded, abandoned or abused children, the handicapped, prisoners, and addicts—for all who are neglected or ignored by society" begin to sound suspiciously insincere. One senses soon that in the humanist philosophy human beings do definitely have differing price tags—and sometimes even lower price tags than certain animals.

Two bizarre incidents occurring in Madison, Wisconsin, some time ago (incidents seeming to be so typical of a university-minded community) brought home to me how inhumane are some of the currents of thought in our society today and how fragile indeed is the so-called value that secular humanists would attach to human lives.

First, Chief, a very popular polar bear at the local zoo, was shot and killed by a police officer when the bear threatened a mentally disturbed man who had crawled his way into Chief's enclosure. Though not yet seriously injured, the man had been struck to the ground by Chief and was in obvious peril. After unsuccessfully trying to lure the bear away from the man, the police officer shot the majestic creature. Understandably, people responded with hurt and frustration. Chief had become an "animal friend" to many. But among the public responses were those (not in the majority, but perhaps reflecting the real feelings of many silent assenters) that suggested that the officer shot the wrong animal.

Not many days later, a young nihilist, also apparently disturbed, released a statement to the press that he intended in a few days to burn a puppy alive on the steps of the university's Memorial Union. His avowed intent was to do something revolting that would stand as a kind of parody of what he considered the heartless, unjust foreign policy of the U.S. government at the time. When hundreds of letters and phone calls poured into the newspaper and humane society offices from near and far, the young man backed down and claimed that his plan was only a bluff. But in the meantime, several people had made open death threats against his life.

I felt heartened at the time to see how many good citizens were ready to become public with their stated affection for two precious creatures of the animal kingdom, a polar bear and a puppy. Indeed, all living creatures and things in the natural order deserve reverence and protection. Yet it was equally disheartening to see the way some people would measure the relative worth of two loveable animals as over against two not-so-easy-to-love, seemingly disturbed individuals. Evidently the bear and puppy claimed priority on the scale of values.

The university philosopher Peter Singer has given some intellectual prominence to the view that there is no radical difference between the value of human lives and the lives of some other animals. Singer believes that to maintain the sanctity of human life over and above all other forms of life is a brand of racism he calls *speciesism*. As an alternative view, Singer suggests that we base our view of what is human on whether the living entity possesses certain characteristics or capacities, such as being able to act intentionally, solve problems, and communicate relationally with other beings. By these criteria, some retarded members of the species *homo sapiens* are nonhuman, while some relatively intelligent adult pigs, dogs, and monkeys are human.

Singer puts it this way, in an essay entitled "Unsanctifying Life":

> Let us say, though just to take an example, that we decide that what is characteristic or distinctive of men and women is a capacity of self-awareness or self-consciousness. Then we will not count severely retarded infants as human beings even though they are clearly members of *homo sapiens;* at the same time we might decide, after examining the abilities displayed by apes, dolphins and perhaps some other mammals, to count these beings as human beings.[1]

> Judged by the characteristics they actually possess, and excluding for the moment such indirect factors as the concerns of parents or others, an infant *homo sapiens* aged six months would seem to be much less a "human" than an adult chimpanzee; and if we consider a one-month-old infant, it compares unfavorably with those adult members of other species—pigs, cattle, sheep, rats, chickens and mice—that we destroy by the millions in our slaughterhouses and laboratories.[2]

The logical conclusion Singer draws from his argument is that either we have to stop killing animals for food and using them for

---

1. Peter Singer, "Unsanctifying Life," *Ethical Issues Relating to Life and Death*, ed. John Ladd (New York: New York and Oxford University Press, 1979), 49.
2. Singer, "Unsanctifying Life," 50.

experiment, or we have to become equally open to the direct mercy killing of retarded infants and even to experimentations on the same. In fact, Singer prefers moving in both directions: placing more restraints on the use and abuse of animal life by people and giving more license to the direct mercy killing of dying, severely retarded, or handicapped people. Says Singer, "Once we see that the case of a dying horse is really quite parallel to the case of a dying infant, we may be more ready to drop the distinction between killing and letting die in the case of the infant too."[3]

Singer's position is a deliberate, conscious rejection of the ancient Christian consensus view on the doctrine of the uniqueness and sanctity of all human life. His is an attempt to replace the Christian ethical and cultural tradition with a secular, humanistic consensus view that would link the notion of value (personhood) not with the relational status of *homo sapiens* to a Creator God, but with certain capacities like self-consciousness and intelligence that may or may not be possessed by certain people and that are in no way possessed only by people. The end result is that the lives of all people are desanctified and the value of any human life becomes a decision left up to the humanistic price-taggers.

Unquestionably, polar bears and puppies do give people considerable personal gratification. And that is good and right. Beautiful creatures such as these deserve public protection, as do trees and lakes and wetlands and baby seals and snail darters and bald eagles. Likewise, however, innocent unborn children and newborns with spina bifida and adolescents with Down Syndrome and adults with mental disturbances and septuagenarians with Alzheimer's are beautiful creatures. They do not become less valuable and even expendable through the public holocausts of abortion or euthanasia in the event that other people's personal pleasures and rights become threatened by their so-called "burdensome" presence.

The following poem was my letter-to-the-editor response to the polar bear and puppy incidents in Madison:

---

3. Singer, "Unsanctifying Life," 53.

Humane Society

Polar bears and playful puppies
please the pampered yippie yuppies.

Den the white, free monarchs
within iceless zoos
for weekend oohs and aahs.

Pen the curious puppies
within cardboard boxes in basement corners
'til animal company is needed
to cuddle the loneliness away.

Fantasizing bearish hugs
and puckering up
for puppy licks and tugs
answers a womb-deep void,
supplies a surrogate
softness and whiteness
when bosom aches
for once-conceptus child
defiled by saline,
incinerated . . . not publicly.

Right of birth brings risk
of messy bahs
and weeklong blahs,
puts a leash on personal pleasure
and dampens fun of springtime protests
for justice.

If *humane's* the name
for loving animals same
as humans,
then let the pups and bears
beware.

> For *animal's* the name
> we give demented men
> we'd sooner shoot than heal,
> and *vegetable's* the same
> for aging ken
> we'd sooner cage and euthanize
> than humanly embrace.

Many other examples could be given of superficial agreements between secular humanists and Christians. They alike resist violent force as a means to resolve human conflict. Both are deeply concerned about racial discrimination, ecological damage, inadequate energy preservation. Both want education to teach more than facts and concepts, but also values. However, the antithesis reaches down into these areas, too.

Consider, for example, the issue of racism and prejudice, so much talked about in the university scene today. At the University of Wisconsin in Madison, a "Covenant on Confronting Racism and Prejudice" was circulated on campus in the early 1990s by the United Religious Workers. It was signed by thousands of students and faculty and was endorsed by the Dean of Students on behalf of the administration. The Covenant read:

> We the undersigned in the Madison and University of Wisconsin community believe in a unique tradition: we continually strive toward an ever greater understanding of our commitment to peace, justice, and equality. We take these words seriously, and believe that they must be pursued with constant, rigorous action. Those ideals, and the strength with which we support them, are our communal pillars of support.
>
> We sign this covenant as a celebration of our beautiful and expressive differences in race, creed, color, religion, gender, and sexual preference.
>
> We sign this covenant as a pledge to speak out when we hear prejudicial words in the community, in the classroom, and in ourselves.
>
> We sign this covenant as a pledge to action—recognizing that words are not enough—to recommit ourselves to active pursuit of our vision for a peaceful, just, and equal world.
>
> As a visible sign of our commitment to this covenant, we will wear/display the Olive Branch button that reads: *Celebrate difference!*

On behalf of a group of Christian students and faculty, I wrote "A Covenant Critique" and submitted it to the offices of the President and the Dean of Students. In it, I suggested some wording for an alternative covenant, which was ultimately accepted (as an alternative) by the United Religious Workers Association, but went unacknowledged by the university administration. This alternative covenant read as follows:

> A *Covenant on Confronting Racism and Prejudice* has been circulating at the University of Wisconsin as well as at various other campuses in the United States. While this covenant seeks with good intention to be embracing of everyone, it does, in a small section of its particular wording, cause some to feel shut out from the broad circle of difference to be celebrated.
>
> The particular statement in the otherwise positive covenant that begs critical response is: "We sign this covenant as a celebration of our beautiful and expressive differences in race, creed, color, religion, gender, and sexual preference."
>
> There are some reluctant nonsigners among us whose creed and/or religion is to believe that not every creed, religion, or sexual preference is to be celebrated and affirmed as beautiful. We wonder, can those covenant affirmers who wish to celebrate difference also celebrate the difference of those of us who religiously and creedally cannot in good conscience celebrate all differences?
>
> It is our very belief system or worldview that requires us to say that not all differences should be declared beautiful. For some creeds, religions, and sexual behaviors are manifestly destructive and threatening to human happiness and survival. Furthermore, the notion of beauty has something of creational normativity in it. A thing or person is beautiful when it/he/she operates in harmony with the created order. Correspondence to creational norms is essential to the very definition of beauty.
>
> Differences of type or appearance which are natural (meaning, existing in a state corresponding to original intent) are indeed beautiful and to be celebrated, such as differences in race, color, and gender.
>
> In our view, there is no act of will, and thus no blame, involved in being Japanese, black, female, American, white, or male. People do not choose race, color, or gender. But it is possible for people to choose creed and religion and to prefer one sexual behavior over another. Those choices, we believe, are not always right choices to be celebrated and described as positively expressive.
>
> A creed that would give license to and even encourage people to "do to others before they do to you" is unacceptable to us, as would be a chauvinistic creed that declares: "Women are chattel and exist purely for the pleasure of men." There are many other unacceptable creedal state-

ments, but we are merely seeking to cite a few examples, not be exhaustive.

A religion or theology that promotes apartheid, or preaches messianic nationalism, or justifies the right to create weapons of destruction powerful enough to annihilate the world is unacceptable to us, no matter which nation makes or possesses them.

Preferences for sexual relations with animals, with small children, with one's own son or daughter, or with persons of the same gender are differences that not all find possible to celebrate.

The *people* holding these views or expressing such preferences are worthy of our non-discriminatory, unconditional love. But we feel uncomfortably compromised to be asked to affirm as beautiful whatever creed, religion, or sexual preference they might follow.

Whatever *is* is not right, true, or good just because it *is* or because it is different.

Our reluctance to sign a covenant celebrating differences of creed, religion, and sexual preference *as well as* the differences of race, color, and gender arises out of a conviction that the first three categories are not as morally neutral as the last three.

However, the right to respect for one's personhood is a right that should apply to all categories. People of all persuasions should seek to protect this right in a pluralistic society.

Therefore, may we respectfully request that full endorsement be given to an alternative (not a substitutionary) covenant confronting racism and prejudice. This alternative covenant would contain all statements in the original except the objectionable paragraph already mentioned, which we suggest should read: *We sign this covenant as a commitment to celebrate nondiscriminately the personhood (unique status and sanctity) of every human being regardless of race, color, gender, or age (natural and nonchoice differences) and regardless of creed, religion, sexual preference, health, or ability (differences that can be but are not necessarily affected by choice).*

Such a change would enable a greater number of people to sign the proposed covenant and join together as allies in the noble cause of defending peace, justice, and equality.

Another popular issue at the university these days is that of environmental stewardship. Here secular humanists and Christians find themselves allied as cobelligerents in many ways, fighting for survival of the natural order. And this is good! But even here, a parting of the ways eventually emerges, as the issue of ecological responsibility comes to impinge on *human* ecology and on the need to alter our sexual lifestyles to forestall disaster to *human* life. The same greed that may lead a farmer to misuse the soil may be what really lies behind the sexual abuse of our bodies, a fact so easily overlooked and even vigorously denied by many secular humanists. Consider, by way of illustration, my poem:

Of Pests and Ecology

The farmer sows his hybrid corn
in last year's weary furrow
of fallen stalks,
reaps it well,
realizes stupendous profit,
and does it again
the following year.

The rootworm beetle, waiting,
lays her eggs,
hopes for second season
of similar corn,
hopes her larva can survive,
thrive as progeny,
now pests to man,
born of greed,
the need for corn . . . money.
A year of soybean
could have spared the soil
of pests and pesticides,
of erosion and tiredness
from human abuse
and overuse.

Pests are a sign,
a rainbow in the soil
of chastening mercy,
of judgment unto grace.
Pests are a pain signal
to the human steward.

Lepers, feeling no pain,
abuse their limbs, unknowingly.

Intemperate farmers disdain to feel it,
prefer instead to anesthetize,
to attack the critters,
to remove the symptoms,
to ignore the root-bound cause,
which is not the worm
but the infested heart
of the pest-killer.

Meanwhile,
at human borough
a lover sows his seed
in the strange, unnatural furrow
of a genderlike mate.
Immunities disappear,
bringing legacy of fear
as another pest is born:
AIDS, a sign of scorn.

Hating this prophetess,
and unwilling to confess
the whole immoral mess,
society screams
for research money
to tame the flame,
clear the name,
extend the game
of pleasured living,
so that partners greedy
for bumper crops
of unlimited sex
at whatever cost
to the soil of human health
can risk erosion
and even extinction
in their pesticide fixation.

Yes, good souls must toil
to repay the soil,

> repair the extremities,
> ransom innocent children
> contaminated by error,
> ostracized by terror.
>
> Indeed, wide hearts don't feint
> to tend the ill, search for healing pill,
> fend off the fear
> of gradual dying
> whether with sinner or saint.
>
> Surely, well spirits bring yield
> of love compost
> to greed-scorched field.
> They visit, too, isolation hells
> of coughing, ghostlike shells sealed
> by fate of death.
>
> But let come the day,
> and come it soon!
> when worms in the land
> and AIDS in the gland
> like pain in the hand
> will be received as messengers
> bidding us plant the soybean,
> reforest the desert,
> reorder the sex,
> nurture the family,
> renew the earth,
> and save from fire
> the fragile flesh
> that is our gift.

Both Christianity and humanism are revolutionary movements. Both speak of themselves as religions and seek to become world encompassing. Both look to the future and see the twenty-first century as pivotal. Both trace their roots far back in history: humanism to ancient China, to classical Greek and Roman culture, to the Renaissance and Enlightenment, and to the modern-day scientific revolution; Christianity to the Hebrew creation story, to the history of the Jewish nation, to the life and teachings of Jesus of Nazareth, and to the history of the Church in its development through ancient, medieval, and modern times. This is an overgeneralization, to be sure, and there has been much positive cross-fertilization through the centuries. However, as worldviews that attempt to explain meanings and origins and destinies, these two remain radically different religions.

The major difference between these two worldviews or religions is essentially this: Radical humanism claims that humankind is the measure of all things and that faith in God is illusory and irrelevant at best and harmful to the future prospects of human happiness at worst. The moral outflow of this view is that humans must contextually create their own values out of their own unqualified freedom and with no supernatural warrants or guarantees. This is *relativism!* It is the belief that there is no moral constant. There are no gods out there, no moral absolutes, no ethical givens. From each situation to the next, people must freely determine anew how they are to act as moral agents.

However, people are really not able to live with this kind of radical discontinuity. They have to have some basis upon which to make their decisions of right or wrong. They have to find some justification for their behavior. They have to find something to fill in for the true root-unity of their life, which they lost when they rejected the special revelation of God as their source of understanding. They look about, above, within, and behind themselves for an integrator to their existence and notice that their temporal existence manifests a great diversity of aspects. They see such creaturely magnitudes as nation, economics, number, law, the community, or the individual. All of these are particular areas of the created order, relative aspects of the whole of reality. When they take one of those aspects and lift it out of context and elevate it to the level of ultimacy, then they make it into an *-ism* or into "the vehicle of an entire philosophy." It may be nationalism, or hedonism, or socialism, or communism, or individualism. Whatever it is, it is a species of the genus relativism.

On the university campus, relativism takes many shapes. In the English department it may take the shape of *deconstructionism*, described and critiqued in my poem entitled "Really!"

Really!

If poems, like prose, undressed,
reveal but naked nouns and verbs,
and pose each moment a face
the opposite first supposed;
if word meanings topple
when nudged by existence and social consensus,
then sense falls into nonsense.

Sweet plums become bitter herbs;
dogs become as psychic as cats,
as flighty as bats,
and fetal lives are less like humans
than hatched bluebottle flies
sitting on manure pies.

Then white blends into black,
female pales into male,
good echoes evil,
essence mirrors fantasy.

And I am slave to be
whatever: knave or preacher,
creature or Creator,
as are professors to be professors or peacocks
who may as well sport porcupine quills
as shimmering feathers.

But, esteemed critic,
is it a sidewalk
your feet touch
as you step the journey at day's end
from your conservatory of letters and meanings
to common house with numbered door?
Or are you merely this moment
head-hopping on purple, poached eggs
in a downward spiral
from your laboratory to your cave?

Contrary to relativistic humanism, where the only absolute is the human self, radical Christianity claims that God is the measure of all things and that earthly and heavenly fulfillment for humans is contingent upon a right religious (heart) response to God's Word revelation. That revelation is descriptive of people's creation out of nothing by divine fiat, of their fall into sin through Adam, and of their and all creation's salvation in and through God's Son, Jesus Christ.

The moral outflow of this theistic view is that God has established an unchanging moral law for the universe, which can be perceived in the natural order by human reason, but which can be known and practiced in its deepest loving intent only through a living faith commitment to Jesus Christ and a radical obedience to the Word of God infallibly recorded in Scripture.

The import of this address is not to suggest that a radical, theistic Christian perspective should replace a secular, relativistic humanism as the predominant worldview at the public university. Not to mention that this is not going to happen, but neither should Christians seek to make it happen, even if it were realistically possible. But it isn't asking too much to demand from university boards, administrators, and faculties that there come to be more openness to true justice in education where a comprehensive pluralism is allowed structurally to exist. Theism and Christianity have a right and responsibility to recapture some space in the forum of ideas. Let the contrasting worldviews compete openly in the educational marketplace!

Perhaps whole separate colleges, under the umbrella of the university system and with the funding of tax-subsidy money, should be established where students could exercise their right to an education according to the dictates of their own conscience, be it theistic, pantheistic, nihilistic, naturalistic, atheistic, or whatever. How would such a true *multi*versity be anywhere near guilty of establishing a certain religion? As the situation now exists, the only religion that has the green light in public education, from preschool to doctoral award ceremony, is the religion of secular humanism.

But is this educational justice? Or is it the tyranny of a particular worldview? Should not education in a democracy be inclusive and pluralistic? But can it be such without allowing to the table of learning many assumed beginnings of thought, such as, in the beginning reason, or in the beginning language, or in the beginning beauty, or in the beginning matter or energy or number or biology—or some combination of any or all of these? And would not true pluralism and inclusiveness allow to the table as a beginning axiom of thought such assumptions as: in the beginning God, or in the beginning the Word, or in the beginning spirit or Spirit or soul or All-Soul? None of the above-listed beginning points can be proven *a priori*. They can only be proven *a posteriori* by the sense they make of all of the phenomena in the middle.

I, as a Christian theist, take as my starting point a personal Creator God. I do so by faith. For others, their starting point may be matter or energy or number or something else. But also by faith! They have to begin or they can't proceed. And so do I! I grant them their beginnings. Can they grant me mine? Or do their beginnings somehow have more provability, less mystery about them? Is my beginning the only faith-based beginning, in their opinion, and thus not deserving of a place in the common marketplace of learning? Is this educational justice?

The secular university is no friend to Christianity. Though a celebration of diversity is a value promoted and pushed there, this celebration turns into censure amounting to hostile opposition when it comes to Christianity, especially of the orthodox or evangelical variety. Any ideas are welcome to the university roundtable of discussion, including religious ideas, as long as those ideas make no exclusive claims to truth. Any truth claims that aspire to a level of ultimacy are viewed as hateful, judgmental, and discriminatory and are ruled out of bounds in academic discussion. The sifting and winnowing of ideas to which academia aspires stops when ideas appear that claim that certain other ideas are false.

In a relativistic universe, no idea may trump another, no religion another, no truth another. Unless the bearers of any ideas admit to the relativity of their ideas and all truth claims, they cannot be invited to the table of learning by the intolerant disciples of tolerance.

So no space can be given in the secular university to any teacher who would advocate for his or her right to teach a course in Christianity and do so from a confessional rather than a comparative religions basis or who would seek to introduce theistic perspectives (with any exclusive truth claims) into the study of any of the disciplines of learning.

Unless Christians of influence are willing to work for and effect structural change that will bring true justice in education, Christianity will continue to exist on the margins of the university, and public education on all levels will be completely controlled by the secular humanists. To compound the problem even more, the failure to effect structural change bringing true justice in education will result in placing Christian education, especially at the college and seminary level, in the exclusive hands of professors who have received their doctoral certifications from universities that embrace secular humanism as their exclusive religion of choice. Though such a result is not inevitable, and monastic retreat for rediscovery of one's Christian roots is not out of the question for those who would be bold enough to cut their ties more radically from the stranglehold public education has upon them, very few voices seem to be urging us in that direction. So the expectant eyes of God directed both at the great university institution and now also at the Christian Church, will still be dappled with tears.

6

Our Culture of Impermanence and Our Unchanging God

God had his fill with the oppression of his people by the Egyptians. Four hundred years was enough suffering. He had seen the affliction of his people and had heard their cry. And now he was ready to deliver them out of the hand of the Egyptians and lead them by a deliverer to a land flowing with milk and honey.

So he appeared one day to Moses, in dramatic fashion at a burning bush, and called him to bring forth his people. At first, Moses protested:

> "If I come to the people of Israel and say to them, 'The God of your ancestors has sent me to you,' and they ask me, 'What is his name?' what shall I say to them?'" God said to Moses, "'I AM WHO I AM." He said further, "Thus you shall say to the Israelites, 'I AM has sent me to you.'" God also said to Moses, "Thus you shall say to the Israelites, 'The LORD, the God of your ancestors, the God of Abraham, the God of Isaac, and the God of Jacob, has sent me to you': this is my name for ever, and this is my title for all generations. Go and assemble the elders of Israel, and say to them, 'The LORD, the God of your ancestors, the God of Abraham, of Isaac, and of Jacob, has appeared to me. . . .'" (Exodus 3:13–16a)

Suppose that God had said to Moses, "I am becoming who I am." This would make God incomplete, inadequate, not fully sufficient. He would not be infinite in his attributes or capacities to meet our needs. He would be a God with great potential.

Or suppose that God had said to Moses, "I am who I am becoming." This would mean that God is in process. He is changing. What we knew him to be last year is no longer true this year. He would be an existential God. He would be a God who merely mimics the very culture of impermanence of which we are a part. David Wells speaks of this culture of impermanence in his significant book *No Place for Truth*. In contrasting the premodern world of an early American Puritan town with our own postmodern era, which Wells calls "Our Time," he says:

> That world prized permanence; ours knows that change is irresistible and has come to need it. They made houses and shoes to last; we build obsolescence into many of our products, and our houses last only about forty years. The deluge of new products that our productive economy has spewed forth itself generates a need that advertisers say will be satisfied only by a fresh purchase....[1]

> Men's socks used to be darned and shirt collars and cuffs turned to make them last longer. Now we simply replace them. And we exchange our homes on the average of once every seven years. We are an astonishingly mobile people. In any given year, about 20 percent of Americans move somewhere....[2]

> There is a sense of impermanence above our lives even as there is within our lives. The norms, values, and principles that were once seen to be enduring absolutes, along with the knowledge of God in which they were grounded, now seem quite uncertain and perishable, anything but the markers that once provided safe moral passage through life....[3]

> They had little that was new; we have little that has persisted. This is true of things, relationships, and values.... They were permanent residents. We are nomads, perpetual immigrants.... Their world was permanent because they knew God to be unchanging; ours is impermanent and God seems largely to have disappeared....[4]

> What is most remarkable about modern people is that they are not in scale with the world they inhabit informationally and psychologically. They are dwarfed. And they have been emptied of their metaphysical substance; more precisely, it has been sucked out of them. There is nothing to give height or depth or perspective to anything they experience. They know more, but they are not necessarily wiser. They believe less, but they are not more substantial. They are attuned to experience and to appearances, not to thought and character.[5]

---

1. David F. Wells, *No Place for Truth* (Grand Rapids: Eerdmans, 1993), 42.
2. Wells, *No Place*, 42–43.
3. Wells, *No Place*, 44.
4. Wells, *No Place*, 46.
5. Wells, *No Place*, 51–52.

Wells readily admits that he is antimodern, that he is not a person of "Our Time." What is this essence of modernity that he rejects? Several things. The essence of modernity is:
1. An addiction to change.
2. An urban consciousness that reduces values down to the lowest common denominator to fit the masses.
3. A consciousness that is attuned to experience and appearances, not to thought and character. Contemporary heroes are celebrities, entertainers, and super-athletes; they are models, but often not model persons.
4. A psychologizing of life that "undermines the desire and capacity to think" and that "identifies access to reality with subjective experiences rather than objective thought."[6]
5. A fascination with technology as a means to unlimited improvement.
6. A love affair with power and a betrayal of the two other sinews that have held Western society together, namely authority and tradition. In a generation of rapid change, of future shock, of accelerated obsolescence of computers and communication systems and clothing styles and nearly everything else, tradition has very little meaning. Tradition isn't a hated word; it is a strange word. Even the concept of tradition has become obsolete. Change is in. Not to go with the flow is to be a cultural nerd. If it's new and innovative, it has to be better! So with religion as well. Shop around at the various style shows until you've found what suits your yen for just the right contemporary look or feel. This may lead you to Evangelical praise gatherings, or Zen Buddhist meditation retreats, or New Age mystic encounters. It may lead to a television screen, a temple, a crystal cathedral. It could lead to a Christian minister, but also to some other high priest: to a medium or psychic, a swami or guru, a channeler or a faith healer, a Christian rock star, a tarot card reader, a psychiatrist, a hypnotist, a Scientologist, a holistic health practitioner, an acupuncturist, a biofeedback specialist, a chiropractor, a Gestalt therapist, a Quantum physicist, a Wicca goddess, or a Gnostic shaman. If the religious shrine happens still perchance to be a traditional-

---

6. Wells, *No Place*, 181.

looking Christian church, it had better not, in fact, *be* traditional. Better for the tastes of some if it be revolutionary, radically feminist, and liberationist. Better for the tastes of others if it be charismatic, sensate, and performist.

7. A loss of religious assumptions to sustain the culture. Life in modernity has been stripped of the divine. What little remains of the divine has been relocated in the private realm. As Richard Neuhaus put it, the public square is naked.

The effect of all of this has been quite dramatic on the Church, including the evangelical wing of it:

a. Christian leaders are becoming "amicable partners" with rather than "cognitive dissidents" within culture.[7]
b. Ministers are becoming professionals who manage by technique rather than truth, who are more psychologists and managers than they are "brokers of truth."
c. Clergy and laity alike are becoming largely disinterested in theology.
d. Learning has been democratized to a "middling standard."[8] There has been a dumbing down of the Church.
e. Absolutes are perishing and are being replaced by a human subject who acts individualistically as a definer of reality and morality.
f. Biblical revelation has been contextualized to the point that critical chicanery and the new hermeneutics have swamped the field of biblical interpretation.
g. Decisions based on tradition and authority and consensus, reached over centuries of prayer and dialogue by God's people waiting on the Spirit, have been replaced by power politics and majority votes taken by Church assemblies and synods that flip-flop their pronouncements year to year.
h. Piety is now measured by how good one feels about him/herself.
i. Therapeutic models of salvation are replacing repentance models, and anthropocentric (people-centered) preaching is replacing theocentric (God-centered).

Perhaps, like Wells, I am not truly a person of "Our Time," for my God hasn't changed and he certainly hasn't disappeared! He who is

---

7. Wells, *No Place,* 136.
8. Wells, *No Place,* cf. 193–98.

my LORD is the I AM WHO I AM, thus not in process, not part of the frustrating cycle of turnover. He is who he is—forever! We can rely on him. He is dependable, trustworthy, consistent. In a world of constant flux, one thing, at least, doesn't change: the caring, attentive eye of our Shepherd LORD upon us. His love never wavers; his concern knows no pattern of fluctuation. His counsel of truth is reliable and steady. The LORD is a Rock, a place to stand that doesn't shift under our feet. He gives height, depth, and perspective to our experience. He gives us the wisdom that transcends information; he gives us the thought and character that transcends experience and appearances.

In a moment of quiet meditation, I was pondering that wonderful thought of God's unchangeability and ended up writing the piece that follows:

I AM

I
LORD,
Is there
anywhere
anything
that lasts?

Longer than the
bright sun
splendidly
rising up
each day?

Longer than the
North Star
standing fixed
in the far-
off sky?

Longer than the
deep blue
glacier ice

settling for
ages?

II

Each crystal of snow
is unlike any other
ever made,
but once fallen
it is changing,
dissolving from the moment
its unique design
is barely set.

So it is
with all that's finite
of things
and creatures
and people.

Not a season goes by
but that in some place
a bird is on the fly
to another home.
Not a day passes
but that in some place
a dying is underway:
a child with cancer breathes her last;
a pet dog is put to sleep;
a shirt is torn for rags;
a car is scrapped for parts;
a house full of memories is razed;
letters, newspapers, and *Time* magazines are burned
or returned
for recycling
into something else
to be used
for the briefest of moments.

Coming and going,
beginning and ending,
always becoming
what one is
or being
what one is becoming
but never being
what one is—
this is the lot
of we people
who people
the earth.

Our dying begins
the moment of our birthing.

And since this is
the transient sense of our lives,
we are never just there,
just the same,
permanent residents,
unchanging,
everlasting,
but always perpetual immigrants,
always in process
from one stage of becoming
to another moment of being—
which is gone
before we can say what it is,
for the moment we can say its name
or define its meaning,
society changes it all.

III
LORD,
Is there
someone,
something,

anything,
anywhere—
any truth,
any right—that is
what it is
and does not
move a hair
in space
or change a mite
from the place
it was to be
from eternity?

....

*Before Abraham was
I AM,
said He,
who is
Yahweh,
and was
the God of our Fathers,
and is to be
the God of our children's children.*

*I am the way,
the fixed North Star,
and what I say
is truth,
still truth,
and always truth,
for not a day
do I, like the sun,
stand still
or like the ancient ice
move far
from where I stood
in the beginning.*

*My sure word does not change;
my perfect law has no range
on which it roams,
however slow.*

*My truth is revealed text,
not begging from context
a redefinition
by moderns
whose values, amphibious,
are as apt to stand (a pretext!)
on solid land
as they are to drift
in a sea of experience.
My statutes are of stone,
not celluloid-blown
by each age in love
with its own
new packaging.
My gift, unembossed,
stands long after
the gift wrap is tossed
away.*

*I am
who I am
who I am,
the same* LORD
*from beginning
to end.
This is my name
forever.*

*I am
the God of Abraham,
the God of Isaac,
the God of Jacob,
the God of ancients,*

*medievals,
and moderns.*

*Fashions come
and fashions go;
passions ebb
and passions flow;
cultures rise
and cultures fall,
but through it all
I repeat my call
and say:
trust me, my child,
and obey.
I'll help you
to be
what I've said
you are.
I'll give you
a name
that doesn't change
or fade from memory.*

*I'll light your path
with truth that's truth
and set your course
with right that's right
and refresh your soul
with waters running down,
forever pure
and living.*

    J. I. Packer, in his significant book *Knowing God*, has identified six things in God that do not change:[9]

1. God's *life* does not change. He is *"from everlasting"* (Psalm 93:2). *"It is he alone who has immortality"* (1 Timothy 6:16).

---

9. J. I. Packer, *Knowing God* (Downers Grove: InterVarsity, 1973), 67–72.

2. God's *character* does not change. In the words of Packer, "Strain, or shock, or a leucotomy, can alter the character of a man, but nothing can alter the character of God. In the course of a human life, tastes and outlook and temper may change radically: a kind, equable man may turn bitter and crotchety; a man of good-will may grow cynical and callous. But nothing of this sort happens to the Creator. He never becomes less truthful, or merciful, or just, or good, than He used to be. The character of God is today, and always will be, exactly what it was in Bible times."[10] Exodus 34:6–7 reinforces this thought: *"The LORD passed before him and proclaimed, 'The LORD, the LORD, a God merciful and gracious, slow to anger, abounding in steadfast love and faithfulness, keeping steadfast love for the thousandth generation, forgiving iniquity and transgression and sin, yet by no means clearing the guilty. . . ."*
3. God's *truth* does not change. *"The LORD exists forever; your word is firmly fixed in heaven"* (Psalm 119:89). *"Long ago I learned from your decrees that you have established them forever"* (Psalm 119:152). *"The grass withers, the flower fades; but the word of our God will stand forever"* Isaiah 40:8).
4. God's *ways* do not change. God does not change his way of salvation, his determination to punish, his way of chastisement, his respect for our prayers and decisions, his infrequent use of miracles, his strategy of power through suffering, his strategy of peace through the efficacy of the once-for-all sacrifice of Jesus Christ on the cross.
5. God's *purposes* do not change. God will not stop building a Kingdom of righteousness, renewing the creation in anticipation of the new heavens and earth, calling a people to himself and restoring them to holiness, after the likeness of Jesus Christ.
6. God's *Son* does not change. Jesus Christ, says the writer of Hebrews is *"the same yesterday, today and forever"* (Hebrews 13:8).

Against the backdrop of human brevity, ephemerality, and vulnerability in the face of God's chastisements, it is wonderfully reassuring to know that Jesus Christ is the same yesterday and today and forever! Jesus, the Son of God, God in the flesh, the eternal heavenly sacrifice, the ultimate high priest and mediator

---

10. Packer, *Knowing God*, 69.

between God and man, is truly the pearl of great price; he truly is the ultimate treasure; he truly is the end-all and be-all of life; he truly is more to be sought after and valued than even life itself.

Everything else is in process. It is changing, subject to mold and moths and rust and the ravages of time. But Jesus Christ is God and the risen Lord, and he remains the same. And whoever receives his Spirit into their heart by faith takes on a borrowed immortality and a changeless significance.

I conclude my thoughts on the immutability of God in a mutable world with a quotation from the Psalms and with a poem from my journal. Psalm 62:6 reads, "He alone is my rock and my salvation, my fortress; I shall not be shaken." My poem "Spray on a Rock," which follows, traces the journey of a drop of water from ocean to cloud to mountain leaf to river back to the ocean. It raises the question: Am I not more than this drop of water? Is my existence but a fatal, cyclical journey? Or, as a person, am I more significant, and can I find a source of permanence and meaning?

Spray on a Rock

I needed a moment to ripple free
from torrential rush of daily existing
and founder down to think and cry;
in crystal cascades of my tears,
to see in new dimension
the tragic flowing of my years.

My push was to the sea, that great
resurgent womb from which I rose,
a drop, ordained to strike a leaf,
and then a pool, which swiftly joined
with other pools to birth a stream
and wind its way toward the sea
to mother in successiveness
a fresh stream of reflectiveness:
Is life, in fact, no more than this,
to rise and fall, to come and go?
Is there no way to 'scape this flow,
this senseless rush, this mortal drift?

But splashing free at sudden stroke,
I sensed I was not of the spray,
for I could think, and I could cry.
And when the spray had left the Rock,
returning to its natural course,
I saw that I remained: a man,
a man set free to stand in midst
of maelstrom, yet with base enough
to scorn the suck of countercurrents
and whirling gulfs and swirling eddies,
bewildering pools of ideas and actions:
emerging and dying, beginning and ending.

Printed in the United States
76576LV00004B/394-576